The Catholic Disciple

Also by Fr. Bob Bedard, CC

Give God Permission
The Memoirs of Fr. Bob Bedard, CC

We are Called to be Companions of the Cross

Reflections of a Veteran Priest

Evangelization
A Challenge for the Catholic Church

Mary, Mother of Jesus
Why the Controversy?

The Catholic Disciple

Fr. Bob Bedard, CC
Founder of the Companions of the Cross

Published by

COMPANIONS OF THE CROSS
Ottawa, Ontario, Canada

Companions of the Cross

Companions of the Cross
199 Bayswater Avenue
Ottawa, Ontario K1Y 2G5

www.companionscross.org

The Catholic Disciple
by Fr. Bob Bedard, CC

This book was originally published in 1998. This 2012 edition has been revised and checked for accuracy. In particular, complete references have been provided for all quotations from Scripture.

Printed in Ottawa, Canada

Second Edition

Other versions are indicated as follows:

GNB—Good News Bible
JB—Jerusalem Bible
Douay—Douay-Rheims
NABRE—New American Bible Revised Edition
RSV—Revised Standard Version—Catholic Edition
KJV—King James Version
ESV—English Standard Version
NLT—New Living Translation

Design by Shannon Kalyniak

ISBN 978-0-9866457-1-6

"The best thing I've ever done
is turn my life over to the Lord.
That makes me his disciple."

– Fr. Bob Bedard, CC

Contents

CHAPTER ONE

The Father

What better place to start than with God himself—the Eternal Being, the Uncaused Cause, the Unknowable. With the unaided light of reason, we could come to know that God exists outside his creation and is all-powerful. But as to the very nature of God and how God is—Father, Son and Holy Spirit—we could never figure that out. It transcends human reason. In order for us to know and believe the deepest truths about God we have to have revelation. That's what our faith is—revealed religion communicated to us by God himself, through his prophets and, above all, through Jesus, his eternal Son.

The Lord has the capacity to reveal himself to every one of us, provided we are open to hearing what he has to say. The mystery can't be explained fully; it has to be experienced. A great deal of what we are as believers has to do with authentic, spiritual experience. Lots of experiences are spurious, and we have to try to sort them out, but we must not be mistrustful of the experiences themselves, because the very act of God's revealing himself is, for us, an experience.

I'm not talking about emotions. I'm talking about something that happens within the person.

Like the following:

> "I know it's true."
> "How do you know?"
> "I just know."
> "How did it happen?"
> "I've opened myself up to the Lord."

That's how the Lord reveals the mystery of himself.

There are a lot of mysteries about God. In this chapter, I want to talk about the mystery of his love.

Look at the mess we are in! Why did God bother to create us if we were going to be such trouble to him? That's the way God loves. He wants me. Amazing! He loves me. Incredible! He's got a place for me in his heart and in his home. Astounding! How can we explain the love that God has spilled over into creation? He has breathed us forth into existence and here we are—tiny specks in the whole spectrum of the universe—and yet, as the Bible tells us, each one of us is *the apple of God's eye* (Deut 32:10). How can we ever fully understand God?

St. Paul uses the word 'mystery' quite often. In Romans, he speaks of the mystery [Jesus] that has been hidden from all the ages and now revealed to us (*cf.* Rom 16:25-26). In Corinthians, he says, *None of the rulers of this age knew the mystery. If they had known it, they would never have crucified the Lord of Glory* (1 Cor 2:8).

They didn't know the mystery. They didn't recognize Jesus—the Word of God, true God from true God. I don't know the mystery until I open my spirit to receive it. Then it is communicated to me by God himself.

God has given us the wisdom to understand fully the mystery, the plan he was pleased to decree in Christ (Eph 1:9). The mystery has been revealed to us. *The mystery of Christ unknown to men in former ages but now revealed by the Spirit* (Eph 3:4-5). *Pray for me that God may put his words on my lips, that I may make known the mystery* (Eph 6:19). *The mystery hidden from ages and generations past, but now revealed to his holy ones* (Col 1:26).

We become the Lord's holy ones when we open up to him. He still has a lot of work to do with us, but he's in the act of purifying us. Jesus refers to the mystery himself in Mark: *To you* (he is speaking to us here) *the mystery of the reign of God* [*is revealed*] (Mark 4:11). God is Father, Son and Holy Spirit—three persons, one God, one family. We are called into relationships, too, in the natural family, created in the image and likeness of God, the spiritual family. That's the mystery.

I'm really not into astronomy, but I've read a little bit about how the universe is expanding, and how there are galaxies over here and over there. Our own solar system is a mere speck in the whole business. Amazing! What does it mean to me? It's just a hint of the immensity, the majesty, the magnificence, the awesomeness of God, because he himself is greater than what he has called into being. God stands outside his creation, and yet enters into it. Incredible!

Is there intelligent life on other planets? I could be wrong, of course, but I don't think so. I think this is it. What's all that stuff out there for then? Probably so that one day we would discover it, and gasp at the immensity of God. If we are to accept the notion of evolution, imagine God waiting all those billions of years to create mankind. We've only been on the scene for a paltry little time, and all kinds of history has preceded us. God obviously has lots of time and is not bothered by things that last for quite a while. What does this say to us? It says that we should get used to waiting, too.

Although it was a good thing to create us, God has done it in his own time. There's a divine sense of timing that we need to plug into. It's not easy. For me, waiting on the Lord is the most difficult thing that I have to do in trying to follow him.

I figure that most of us are pretty impatient, even if we don't want to admit it. Have we ever had any good ideas? Has the Lord touched our lives? Have we turned things over to God in a lot of ways? Do we have some ideas on how we'd like to serve him? Do we have some good ideas about what the Bishop should do? There are thousands of good ideas. What are we supposed to do with them? We are supposed to wait until the Lord gives us his idea. We are not called to do good things for God; we are called to do God's thing. The Lord will give the vision; we just have to wait.

God created man in his image; in the divine image he created him, male and female he created them (Gen 1:27). The Lord has created us in equal, but distinct roles—male and female. That is reflective of himself and is part of the mystery. The Father has the plan. The Son is the one to interact with creation, and draw it to the Father. The Holy Spirit is the power to get things done.

The Son is obedient and does the Father's will. Jesus didn't seem to know the future unless it was revealed to him by the Father. I don't know how that works. Jesus said, *But as for the day or the hour, nobody knows it, neither the angels of heaven, nor the Son; no one but the Father* (Mark 13:32 JB). The Holy Spirit is obedient as well. Jesus said, *If I fail to go, the Paraclete will never come to you* (John 16:7). The Holy Spirit has come and is available to us now.

One of my prayers every morning is: "Holy Spirit, you are welcome here. Take over—my mind, my will, my body, my spirit, and whatever else I have. Do your work and bring forth the Kingdom of God. Push back whatever is keeping people from opening up to the love of God. Set your people free. Holy Spirit, come and do it."The original plan of God was that we would live in justice and peace, under the original blessing. However, we had other ideas. Sin entered the picture and things fell apart right from the start. Sin is a gloomy topic, but we have to face it.

Sin is basically a rebellion against God. It's wanting to do things our own way, quite apart from what God might want. We all have sinned and done our own thing. That's our participation in the original sin. We can't blame it on anybody. We can't say, "If only Adam and Eve had not sinned..." If they hadn't sinned, then we would have, and would have cut ourselves off from God.

Sin is our downfall. It's like writing God out of the agenda. It's like wresting control away from God and taking charge ourselves. The consequences of that have been incredible, very sad—strife, suffering, illness and death. Have we ever said, "How can God do these terrible things?" or perhaps, "How can he allow this plane crash or allow that typhoon to destroy so many lives?" God doesn't "do" such things. They are all the result of what we have done. The Book of Wisdom says—*God did not make death* (Wis 1:13), and goes on to explain that we have contrived it ourselves because we have decided to do things our own way and ignore God's offer of life. It is we who have chosen something less than life. And this ends up being death and all the things that accompany it—pain, suffering, deprivation.

Sin is our real enemy. It has left us with a weakness, a flawed nature. The fact that we are in a fallen state is not a popular teaching in these days. Some think it's too pessimistic. I don't. I think it's realistic.

I used to give the example of a little baby boy. Everybody loves babies. They're cute. We can pick them up and cuddle them and talk baby talk. If a baby has a rattle in its hand and is cooing and giggling, and we take that rattle away, what happens then? That delightful little soul becomes not so delightful. The hair begins to bristle up and down on the head, the veins stick out, and the cute little chap turns purple and yellow and green. He's selfish by nature.

And where do children at school learn to be cruel? I don't know. I think there's a part of us that's cruel. When I was in elementary school, any new arrival in the middle of the year had to fight his way through two or three bullies before he got respect. Anyone who didn't was as good as dead. It was automatic. New kid in school? Good fights at recess. Where does that come from?

There's something flawed about our nature. To gloss everything over and say—"Oh no, there's no evil. We are all good"—is not going to get us anywhere. Whom are we trying to kid? Notice what St. Paul says of this: *I am weak flesh, sold into the slavery of sin. I cannot even understand my own actions. I do not do what I want to do, but what I hate. The desire to do right is there, but not the power* (Rom 7:14-15, 18). Not having the power is the key. Can we relate to that inner struggle? There's a war going on inside me. I want to do what is right, but I end by doing what's wrong, and I know it's wrong, but I do it anyway? That's sin. That's human. That's the way we are. Sin is a reality.

Are we familiar with the seven deadly sins: envy, covetousness, pride, anger, lust, gluttony, and sloth? Can we relate to any of those? I can. We tend so easily in those directions.

And breathes there anyone more than three years old who has not sinned with the tongue? Listen to what St. James says about it: *All of us fall short in many respects. If a person is without fault in speech, he is a man in the fullest sense because he can control his entire body. When we put bits into the mouths of horses to make them obey us, we guide the rest of their bodies. It is the same with ships. However large they are, and despite the fact that they are driven by fierce winds, they are directed by very small rudders on whatever course the steersman's impulse may select. The tongue is something like that. It is a small member; yet it makes great pretensions. See how tiny the spark is that sets a whole forest ablaze! The tongue is such a flame. It exists among our members as a whole universe of malice. The tongue defiles the entire body. Its flames encircle our course from birth, and its fire is kindled by hell. Every form of life—four-footed or winged, crawling or swimming—can be tamed and has been tamed by mankind, but the tongue no man can tame. It is a restless evil, full of deadly poison* (Jas 3:2-8). Pretty strong language.

Have we ever said anything bad about anybody else? Have we ever said anything bad to anybody else? Have we ever said something and wished we hadn't said it? Have we ever wished we could reach out after we have spoken certain words, retrieve them, and stuff them back into our mouths? I have. Foot-in-mouth disease has been one of my problems for years. Who among us has not sinned with the tongue?

We have all fallen short, but God has not been content to leave us there. He has instituted the classic Operation Rescue. First of all, he called Abraham to himself: *I will be very good to you, and I will make your descendants like the sands of the sea, which are too numerous to count* (Gen 32:13). That was rather unlikely. Abraham was over seventy at the time and he had no offspring. Isn't it just like God to say something which sounds totally impossible, and then make it happen? It is a good lesson for us. If something is unlikely, there's a fair chance it comes from God, because he does some very unlikely things.

God selected the Jewish nation, later known as the Jews, as his chosen people. Why did he pick them? Probably because of all the nations on earth at the time, he could see that they were the most likely to respond to him in a positive way. The Law is not complicated. It's not obscure. It's not difficult. We all know it's wrong to kill. Nobody has to tell us that. It's the same law that is written on the heart of every human being. For Moses it was written on the tablets, to be made more easily understood. God gave his people the Law to rescue them from sin. They were to come into union with him by following the Law. *My lips pour forth your praise, because you teach me your statutes* (Ps 119:171). Psalm 119 is filled with sentiments like that.

People were saved by turning away from sin and turning to God. That's what John the Baptist preached when he came—repentance leading to salvation.

How does it work? We make a conscious decision to turn away from sin and to turn back to God. As we do that, God purifies us, touches us from within, and we know it. That whole dynamic is what happens in the Sacrament of Confession. When a person has sinned, and wants to repent, he celebrates the sacrament, and knows something has happened. Confession can become routine—dry as dust. But it's not supposed to be. Have we had the experience, at least once in our lives, of celebrating the Sacrament of Reconciliation or Penance or Confession and feeling tremendously relieved? I have. What a blessing from God!

God touches the spirit within us and we know it. It's an experience—the divine dynamic. When I began to teach the senior religion program at St. Pius X High School, I was trying to be realistic. I felt that, by and large, the eighteen-year olds weren't at all sure about God. Granted some were quite sure he was real and tried to live that out, but at the other end of the scale were those who were quite sure he didn't exist, or if he did, it didn't matter. In the middle were the great majority who just weren't sure. I used to tell them, "Give God a chance." And I'd quote from Jeremiah: *If you seek me with all your heart, I will let you find me* (Jer 29:13 JB), and Psalm 37: *Commit your [life] to the Lord; trust in him and he will act* (Ps 37:5 ESV). I would say, "God will touch your life if you let him. God will reveal himself to you if you ask him. Give God a chance."

To all who accepted him [Jesus], he gave power to become children of God (John 1:12 JB). He does something. In the Book of Revelation, Jesus says, *Here I stand, knocking at the door. If anyone hears me calling and opens the door, I will enter his house and have supper with him and he with me* (Rev 3:20)—a meal, symbol of friendship.

Day after day, I would drill them. The Lord will deal with you, I would say again and again. Give God a chance, I would repeat. Say, "Lord, if you're real, show me somehow. I need to know."

Some of them began to do that. One of the great consolations of teaching is that sometimes the students will listen. Sometimes they'll even do what the teacher suggests. It makes teaching worthwhile.

I remember one year the seniors had their own retreat. Those who were really firm in their faith set it up and they invited some of their buddies to go.

There was one big fellow, a football player, who used to sit in the last row of the classroom with his chair tipped back, looking at me down his nose, quite skeptical, I thought. He never opened his mouth, never spoke, except to say, "Hi, Father" as he went quickly by. Because a lot of his friends were going on the retreat, he decided he'd go, too. They actually had told him they'd be playing some football as well. He went to play football, but something else happened. He opened his life to the Lord and came back a changed man. I didn't notice it the following Monday as he sat in his regular place at the back. After the class was over and everybody had cleared out, he came over and said, "Father, I want to talk to you." He was a big fellow, about 6'2". Here was this rather large chap looking down at me. I wasn't sure what was coming.

"Father," he opened, "we had a retreat this weekend, and I went on it."

"Yes, I knew that," I replied. (I had had nothing to do with it, but I'm nosey. I had procured the list, and I knew he'd been there.) "How did it go?" I asked.
"Father, it was great," he responded. "It was terrific. Father, you

know those things you've been saying about God and how real he is, and how much he loves us and how close he is, and how he reveals himself to us if we ask him?" He was becoming more animated.

"Yes," I said, "yes, I know the stuff you mean," still not sure where the conversation was going.

"Well," he loomed over me, "it's true."

How did he know? He had just opened his heart to the Lord and the Lord had dealt with him. That's the divine dynamic. Any time we respond to a call from God, the Lord will honour it, and we will know it. I could give fifty more examples of high school students who went through that same process.

A fellow asked Jesus one time: *Teacher, what good must I do to possess everlasting life?* (Matt 19:16) and Jesus told him he knew he'd been a student of the Law and knew what to do. It's really simple, but not easy. We are just to keep the commandments and respond to God. That will do it.

God chose Abraham to be the Father of the Jewish nation, but he tested the man, didn't he? He told him to take Isaac out and sacrifice him on the mountain. Abraham obediently took his own son and was about to do it. Of course, God wouldn't let him. He was testing him. Have we ever been tested? Have we had trials of one kind or other in our own lives, at work, on the job, in marriage, with children, brothers, sisters, parents, with health, with finances? Have we had difficult times? That's par for the course. What did we do in the trial? Did we throw ourselves at the feet of God? That's what he wants. He tests us. I've had lots of trials. I haven't come through them all with flying colours, but I have come through them with his help.

Abraham's grandson, Jacob, had sons of his own: Reuben, Simeon, Levi, Judah, Issachar, Zebulun, Benjamin, Dan, Naphtali, Gad, Asher and Joseph. The sons of Levi became the priests, and the two sons of Joseph, Ephraim and Manasseh, along with the remaining sons of Jacob, became the fathers of the twelve tribes of Israel—the chosen people. God tested Abraham another time by giving him orders to leave his home town, Ur of the Chaldees, and set out for the Promised Land. He was over seventy, but he went anyway and *set out without knowing where he was going* (Heb 11:8 JB). I love that line. That's the way I feel so often. I have no idea of where I am going. Sometimes people will ask: "What's going to happen next?" I haven't got a clue.

The saga of the chosen people was like a roller coaster. When they would fall into line with the plans of God, they would prosper and their society would be at peace. When they began to slip away into sin, they fell apart. Up and down, up and down. One time when the people were sinning and falling away from God, *The Spirit of God possessed Zechariah and he took his stand above them: "Because you have abandoned the Lord," he said, "he has abandoned you"* (2 Chr 24:20). They stoned him to death—the fate of the prophet. Early and often did the Lord send his messengers to them, but they mocked them. They ignored God and despised his warnings. They scoffed at his prophets. Some they even put to death. That was the history of the chosen people.

Sometimes I get the impression that the best thing we do is to divide into camps. When we have different opinions, what's the easiest thing to do? Divide and go our own ways. What's the thing that God wants us to do? Work it out, seek his will, set aside our own agendas, and listen for his. So the Jewish people divided—the kingdom of Israel in the north, and the kingdom of Judah in the south. However, the Lord kept sending his prophets to them and kept calling them back to repentance. *If my people ... humble themselves and pray, and seek my presence and turn from their evil ways, I will hear them from heaven and pardon their sins and revive their land* (2 Chr 7:14). That word holds true today.

When the Canadian Fathers of Confederation in 1867 were over in Westminster waiting for the British Parliament to discuss the whole business of a new country in North America which would be faithful to the Crown, one of the Fathers of Confederation, Leonard Tilley from New Brunswick, said, "I think it should be called a Dominion, because there is a line in Psalm 72, '*His dominion shall be from sea to sea*'" (Ps 72:8 KJV). This land was claimed for Christ by those who came here in the sixteenth century and preached the Gospel to those who were here before them. Very often called the King's or the Queen's Dominion, originally this was the Lord's Dominion of Canada. If only the people could hear and accept that now, what wonders God could do.

This same kind of word was spoken to the Jewish people. *Provided that you and your children return to the Lord, your God, and heed his voice with all your heart and all your soul, just as I now command you, the Lord, your God, will change your lot; and taking pity on you, he will again gather you from all the nations wherein he has scattered you* (Deut 30:2-3). The history of the chosen people had lots of ups and downs. The Assyrians came and laid siege to Jerusalem. They drubbed Palestine from north to south, wiping out towns. At Jerusalem they were turned back by prayer. I remember that poem by Lord Byron with the line:

> The Assyrian came down like the wolf on the fold,
> And his cohorts were gleaming in purple and gold.[1]

The Lord intervened and the enemy was turned back (2 Kgs 18-19). The highs and lows continued and eventually people were carted off into captivity to Babylon in about the year 587 B.C. Later, the King of Persia conquered Babylon, and the chosen people lived in captivity under him. Eventually they were allowed to return, rebuild the temple, and set up their society

1 George Gordon Byron, "The Destruction of Sennacherib," *Hebrew Melodies* (London: John Murray, 1815), p. 46.

once again. The whole story continued. They suffered invasions from Macedonia, and Rome.

Through all that time, out of the mouths of the prophets and the inspired writers, echoed the promise of the one who was to come, the one who would save his people: *The days are coming when I will make a new covenant with the house of Israel and the house of Judah. I will place my law within them, and will write it upon their hearts; I will be their God and they will be my people* (Jer 31:31,33). This, of course, refers to Jesus. He was called the promised one, the anointed one, the long-awaited one, the Messiah, the Christ. He would be rooted in Jewish history, descended from David, born of a virgin in Bethlehem.

There were two apparently opposing pictures of the one who was to come. One pictured him as a victorious king: *I see One like a son of man coming, on the clouds of heaven. He receives dominion, glory, and kingship; nations and peoples of every language serve him. His dominion is an everlasting dominion that shall not be taken away, his kingship shall not be destroyed* (Dan 7:13-14). That's a picture of the glorious Jesus, King of Kings, and Lord of Lords, reigning over all, and was the kind of prophecy most of the people liked to hear.

The people who walked in darkness have seen a great light; and the rod of their taskmaster you have smashed ... For a child is born to us, a son is given us; upon his shoulder dominion rests. They name him Wonder-Counselor, God-Hero, Father-Forever, Prince of Peace (Isa 9:1,3,5).

There was a whole line of prophetic utterances that referred to Jesus as the conquering king, but then there were other things that spoke of him as a suffering servant. *Without beauty, without majesty (we saw him), no looks to attract our eyes; a thing despised and rejected by men, a man of sorrows and familiar with suffering ... And yet ours were the sufferings he carried ... Yet he was pierced through for our faults, crushed for our sins. On him lies a punishment that brings us peace, and through his wounds we are healed* (Isa 53:2-5 JB).

Jesus came as the one who was to save his people from that which bore them down the most—their sins. His message was not popular because people were looking for the glorious conquering king to run roughshod over their enemies. Instead he came as the suffering servant and went to the Cross. That's part of the mystery, too.

The Father sent the Son to earth knowing what was going to happen to him. But it's called love. *God so loved the world that he sent his only Son...* (John 3:16). We can only guess what that cost the Father and the Son—to be separated in whatever way they had to be in order for Jesus to come and be one of us. If I knew that one of my sons was going to get beaten up or killed in the street, would I still send him out? I wouldn't do it. We would call that madness. The Lord calls it love. That's what love is—giving everything away and asking for nothing back.

When Jesus came to earth, it was thought that these prophecies concerning the conquering king and the suffering servant referred to two different people. But, in fact, they didn't. They referred to the same person coming twice: first, as a suffering servant, and then finally (he hasn't returned yet) as the all-conquering king. Are we all looking forward to that? I certainly am. We don't know when it's going to happen, but we'll all be witnesses to it in one way or other. There will be no choice then. Every single human being will recognize Jesus as King. No more alternatives. It won't be up for debate; they won't be discussing it in academic halls, saying, "What do you think? Do you think he is? Do you think he isn't?" There will be no question. All will say he is, whether they like it or not. I'm looking forward to that.

What about all the millions of people who somehow have never heard about him? What about those who lived before Jesus came? Or those who didn't have God dealing with them in the special way that he dealt with the Jews—the Canaanites, the Babylonians, the Egyptians, the Persians? What about the people today who never hear the Gospel? My theory is that there are people right on our own street that have never properly heard the Gospel. It comes over TV, over the radio, in books, on billboards. There are churches all over the place and still there are people here who haven't heard the Word. Why? Because we get in the way. The witness to the Gospel is compromised by our less than perfect witness and they don't really hear it. How can people be saved without hearing the Gospel? The Lord says, *Keep the commandments* (Matt 19:17).

Jesus says: *Try to enter by the narrow gate* (Matt 7:13 JB). Total surrender to Jesus is the narrow gate and the sure way to salvation. It's not so easy though. There's a cost. Somebody came to Jesus and said, *'I will follow you wherever you go'. Jesus answered, 'Foxes have holes and the birds of the air have nests, but the Son of Man has nowhere to lay his head'* (Luke 9:57-58 JB). In other words, "It's not easy to follow me. I want you to know that." The narrow gate is the sure way to salvation, and the best decision we can ever make, but, *My son* (or daughter), *when you come to serve the Lord, prepare yourself for trials* (Sir 2:1). That's a line I can never forget.

One of the things for which I am truly grateful is that the Lord does not expect me to judge anybody else. I have been relieved of that responsibility. He, the Father, has appointed Jesus as Judge. I suspect he's done it that way because Jesus is good at it. I'm delighted not to have to do it. Jesus is the Judge and he is merciful. We just have to leave people to the Lord.

God's plan will go ahead. Jesus said, *I want my house to be full* (Luke 14:23). *There are many rooms in my Father's house* (John 14:2 JB). What does that mean? It means don't worry about being crowded out. There's lots of room around his table in the heavenly Jerusalem, but no place for those who reject God. Frightening, isn't it?

In the meantime, we struggle here on a battlefield. We will be getting into the reality of the spiritual war that's going on around us in detail in Chapter 10. *Satan*, Jesus says, *is a liar and the father of lies* (John 8:44). The father of lies landed on the earth. Why is Satan active here? Because we let him be. Every time we sin, we open the door for the enemy. That's why he's having such a heyday here.

Our sins pile up and become a weight heavy upon the earth and things begin to crack. We need a deliverer, somebody who can save us from the effect of our sins. That's not pessimistic. In fact, it turns out to be very optimistic and positive because the Father has sent the one who can do just that—Jesus, Saviour and Lord—to save us from sin and its effects. He wasn't a political leader. He was the saviour of the world, and as we unite ourselves with him, all of our battles get fought and all our victories are won. Without the death of Jesus, there would be no salvation. None of us would ever have been able to bridge that gulf—between ourselves and the Father who created us—without Jesus. He has done it and salvation has been accomplished.

All of that to say that the Lord has started the ball rolling. He has chosen a people, spoken his Word, and has urged us all to follow him. We could study the Bible from now until whenever and not learn all the lessons that are available there. Centuries passed, and at the appointed hour the turning point of human history arrived in the person of Jesus Christ, our Saviour and Lord. We will talk in the next chapter about him and specifically what he did.

Study Questions:

1 After Fr. Bob experienced renewal in his prayer life, he said, "I began to realize that God has the capacity to enter my life, that the Holy Spirit has the power to change me, to do things in me that I could not do myself." Where do you need the power of the Holy Spirit in your life?

2 Having read Chapter 1, what are some of the ways God has revealed his love for you through Jesus?

3 The Father tells us in Deuteronomy 32:10 that we are *the apple of his eye*. Meditate on this amazing truth and express your gratitude to the Father with the following prayer used by Fr. Bob:

Father, I place myself in your presence now as I pray. You have called me to life. Thank you for this and for all your other many blessings. I worship you as the God of heaven and earth, my Creator and my Father. Help me to change in my life whatever needs to be changed. I confess my sinfulness before you (pause and silently specify).

I ask you to enter my life in a new and deeper way. I want to know you as a person. Please give me the faith that I need to experience your presence in my life. Thank you, my Lord, for answering my prayer. Amen.

CHAPTER TWO

Jesus

Our coming to terms with Jesus is at the central core of what God wants to do in our lives. He has sent his Son who has purchased life for us at a tremendous cost. Jesus is the Saviour. The very name 'Jesus' means in Hebrew 'God saves'. Coming to terms with him on an individual basis is the essence of our faith and where we start if we want to live it out.

Our faith is not so much membership in the Church, although that is important. It is not so much following God's rules and guidelines, the commandments, although that obviously is important, too. But, most important of all, it is a relationship with a person—Jesus Christ, the Son of the living God.

The tomb was empty. He was raised glorious from the dead and *lives now to make intercession for us* at the Father's right hand (Heb 7:25). Together with the Father, he sent the Holy Spirit (topic of the next chapter).

One of the Holy Spirit's basic tasks is to witness to our spirits who Jesus is. Jesus lives, and we can know him as a living person. We have to come to terms with Jesus, talk to him. We can say something like: "Jesus, I hear that you are alive. I want to open my heart to you. You said, 'All who laboured and were burdened should come to you.' I want to do that. If you have really risen, if you really are alive, then show me. I'll do whatever you say." God speaks to the heart. If we come to terms with him, he will touch us. If we open our hearts to the Lord, he will deal with us.

Jesus Christ is the long awaited one, the one spoken of in the Psalms and by the prophets, the anointed one, the Messiah, the Christ, the one who was to come, the one who would set his people free. We celebrate his coming each Christmas. The turning point of human history was the day that Jesus Christ came to earth and became one of us. All of history revolves around that.

As I have pondered and prayed over it, the fact that not only has Jesus become one of us, but also that he remains one of us, amazes me. He will always be fully human while remaining fully divine. God wanted us to be part of his family so badly that he sent Jesus to be one of us. It is a profound mystery, and never ceases to baffle me.

Jesus came, and he was much more than was anticipated. It was not expected that he would be who he really was—the eternal Son of God, begotten by the Father from all eternity. The Lord, by the way, is the Lord of the unexpected. We have to be ready to be surprised.

A few years ago, just before a weekday morning Mass, the lights suddenly went out all over the district. The chap who was leading the Rosary said "Let's ask Our Lady to get the lights on in time for Mass." Two minutes before Mass they came on—just like that. I wanted to make some comment about the lights, so at the beginning of the homily I said something about the lights that was reasonably humorous. A few people snickered.

I find that at nine in the morning, people don't laugh much at anything. Then I said, "I didn't say it at the beginning of Mass, because, if I had, you wouldn't have heard me, not because I wasn't speaking loudly enough, but because you weren't expecting me to say anything, and so you wouldn't have been listening. You usually listen to the homily. The rest is in the book. It is the same thing at the end of Mass. We are not expecting anything different." Nevertheless, at the end of Mass, I made some other comment. I forget what I said. Even I wasn't listening. When I got to the back, one fellow came up and said, "What did you say at the end there? I didn't catch it."

The point I'm trying to make is that we have to be listening to the Lord, not just at daily Mass, but continually, in our waking hours. He is the Lord of surprises. If we are not tuned in, we will miss so many things the Lord is doing and saying.

In the beginning was the Word, and the Word was with God, and the Word was God... (John 1:1 JB). Isn't that an odd description—"the Word"? But what is the expression of any idea? A word. Jesus is the expression of the Father's fullness. So he is the Word of God. *And the Word was made flesh and dwelt among us* (John 1:14), or literally: "pitched his tent among us." *God so loved the world that he sent his only begotten Son, that whoever might believe in him would not die, but have eternal life* (John 3:16).

We can only guess what it cost the Father to be separated from the Son. The Father knew we were going to abuse his Son and eventually put him up on a cross, and yet he sent him anyway. And that is called love.

The way God loves is total. He gives with no strings attached. His love is unconditional, asking nothing back. No matter what we do, his love will never change. Never. There is nothing that we can do to make God love us any less and he can't love us any more than he does. He loves us fully and completely. That's the way God loves us—no conditions, total, full acceptance. He calls us out of sin because he loves us, and his love will never change.

Referring to Jesus, St. Paul writes: *For in him, the whole fulness of deity dwells bodily* (Col 2:9 RSV). Jesus is truly God. Paul says again: *He is the visible likeness of the invisible Father* (Col 1:15 GNB). Jesus himself makes the same point in a reply to the Apostle Philip: *If you have seen me, you have already seen the Father* (John 14:9 JB).

The scary thing is that Jesus calls us to be one with him the way he and the Father are one: *Lord that they might be one, as you and I are one, so that the world will know that you have sent me* (John 17:21 NLT).

There is a depth of meaning here. If we can come together in unity of mind and heart, and move together at the Lord's bidding and command, fantastic things will happen. It takes a daily decision to bury a lot of our own priorities and agendas and preferences, so that the Lord himself can work through us. It's not easy.

In the early Church, the people sang songs when they gathered to celebrate the Eucharist and at prayer gatherings. There were hymns such as this: *Though he [Jesus] was in the form of God, he did not deem equality with God something to be grasped at. Rather, he emptied himself... being born in the likeness of men. He was known to be of human estate... he humbled himself, obediently accepting even death, death on a cross... so that at Jesus' name every knee must bend... and every tongue proclaim to the glory of God the Father: Jesus Christ is Lord* (Phil 2:6-11). We don't know what tune they sang it to, but the song speaks clearly about Jesus' divinity. It is amazing how people can read the Scriptures, believe they have the Word of God, and still not believe Jesus is divine. *The reflection of the Father's glory [he is], the exact representation of the Father's being* (Heb 1:3).

In the Book of Revelation, John, the visionary, describes what he sees: *One like a son of man wearing an ankle-length robe and a golden sash, with long white hair, eyes of fire, feet of brass, voice like the roar of rushing waters* (Rev 1:13 paraphrase). That is Jesus, of course, but the images—the white hair, the sash, the robe—come out of the Jewish Scriptures (*cf.* Dan 7:9, 13) where they are used to describe God alone—yet another affirmation of the divinity of Jesus. *Worthy is the lamb... to receive honour and glory and praise* (Rev 5:12). Jesus is the Lamb of God. Note that the next verse says, *To the one seated on the throne, and to the lamb, be praise and honour, glory and might, forever and ever!* (Rev 5:13). The praise accorded to Jesus is equal to that given to the Father.

We have to come to terms with Jesus. He has to mean something to each of us. That's the Father's plan. *To all who did accept him he gave power to become children of God* (John 1:12 JB). We have to open up to him, to let him in. *I stand at the door and knock. If anyone hears my voice and opens the door, I will come in and eat with him, and he with me* (Rev 3:20 NIV).

Jesus is the obedient one, the one who saves, who always does the Father's will because he knows that there is nothing more important than that. We have to get into that as well. The will of God is the only thing worth doing in this world, the only thing that ultimately works anyway.

Jesus says: *My food is to do the will of the one who sent me and to complete his work* (John 4:34 JB). *My aim is to do not my own will, but the will of him who sent me* (John 5:30 JB). And one of my favourite lines of Scripture: [*The Son does*] *only what he sees the Father doing* (John 5:19 JB). Could we be like that—doing only what we see the Father doing? Let's say to him: "Lord, we want to come before you in repentance and get away from sin. We want to come before you and surrender. We want to come before you in total availability. We don't want to stand in your way. Do what you want to do. You have our permission."

A good strategy for ministry would be to watch and see what God does, and then do it with him. That's what Jesus did. He would go to the towns and preach the Good News. He would touch and heal the sick, and the crowds would gather. The next morning he would get up early and pray—commune with his Father—outside town where it was quiet. The disciples would get up a little later. They hadn't got into praying in the early morning as yet. And they'd go looking for him, find him outside town, and say, "Rabbi, so there you are. Come back to town. Things are really looking good today. You should see the crowd searching for you! Fantastic!" That was the logical thing to do—go where the crowd was. All the while, they would be saying to themselves: "This is the beginning of the big movement to set Israel free." And Jesus would reply: "No, I must go on to other towns because that is the will of the one who sent me." How did he know? He knew because he consulted with his Father. He communed with him every morning. The Father honoured the things that Jesus did in obedience to him.

As I see it, Jesus' mission in the world is five-fold:

1. To proclaim the Good News

Jesus' mandate was to go to the house of Israel and proclaim the Good News, and this is exactly what he did. Those who followed after him would go to the whole world. Repent. Turn away from sin. Get back to God. Believe in the Gospel. Believe in me. The Kingdom of God is among you (*cf.* Mark 1:14).

Do we understand what the Kingdom of God is? The Kingdom of God is fully accomplished in heaven. In that sense it is coterminous with heaven. But that's not the only place where the Kingdom of God exists. The Kingdom of God can exist here. Don't we say in the Our Father, "Thy Kingdom come...on earth as it is in heaven"? The degree to which we are doing the Father's will is the degree to which the Kingdom of God is being realized in us. Believe the Good News. *The Kingdom of Heaven is close at hand,* Jesus would say (Matt 3:2 JB). Making the Kingdom of God come on earth is the work of the Holy Spirit.

Jesus calls for a response. *I am the Way, the Truth and the Life...* (John 14:6 JB). He didn't say: I see the way. He didn't say: I know the way. He said, *I am the way* (John 14:6). *Follow me* (Matt 9:9). *I am the light of the world* (John 8:12). *I am the bread of life. No one who comes to me shall ever be hungry, and no one who believes in me shall ever thirst* (John 6:35).

Luke says, *There is no salvation in anyone else, for there is no other name... by which we are to be saved* (Acts 4:12). Jesus is the one. Jesus himself says, "*Try to [enter] through the narrow gate* (Luke 13:24). That's himself; he is the narrow gate. *I am the gate of the sheepfold*, he says (John 10:7 JB). Come through me. It's not easy entering through the narrow gate, but it is the sure way to salvation. We go through Jesus. We make a total commitment to him and try to live that out.

The Good News proclaims a fullness of life. *I have come*, Jesus says, *that they might have life and have it to the full* (John 10:10). He promises a fullness of peace. My *peace is my gift to you, not as the world understands it, but my peace* (John 14:27 paraphrase). He speaks of a fullness of joy. *I have told you this so that my own joy may be in you and your joy be complete* (John 15:11 JB).

2. To do the works of God

Jesus healed the sick, and the crowds came. If we want to draw a crowd, we simply have to heal the sick. *Vast crowds kept following him because they saw the signs he was performing for the sick* (John 6:2). The afflicted sought him out, because he could remove their afflictions.

Healings, deliverances, exorcisms, miracles—he did them all. They would say, "Never have we seen the likes of this! This must be from God" (*cf.* Mark 2:12). And many would be convicted through seeing the signs at work. The signs were intended to catch the attention of men and women to authenticate the word that he was speaking. *If you refuse to believe in me, at least believe in the work I do...* (John 10:38 JB).

Healing bodies is easy. Healing minds and emotions is a little more difficult. Healing souls and spirits is the most difficult of all. It is the best work that God does. He touches hearts.

I taught high school as a priest for twenty years. I tried mightily to touch the hearts of my students. I never did. When I began to turn things over to the Lord, he began to touch their hearts, and they began to change before my eyes. It was a marvelous work. I have seen people healed of physical ailments, and that's great, but the greatest work that God does is to touch a heart, capture it, and grapple it to himself. That's the thing I want to see most. I can't do it. I can only root him on. Go for it, Lord! Get out there and do it!

When I pray in the morning, one of the things I do is something I call 'The Holy Spirit Roll': "Holy Spirit reign. Holy Spirit rule. Holy Spirit roll. Roll on out there. Roll up and down those streets. Pound on those doors. Get in there. Capture those hearts."

Only God can capture a heart. It's marvelous. I don't know how he does it. It's grace. We do our bit. We speak the words. We try to live it out. We try to witness to the Gospel. We celebrate it. We do what we're supposed to, and it all comes under the heading of evangelization. Speaking it, giving it out—that's our work. Conversion—that's God's work. That's a grace. We can't manufacture grace. God gives it. It's amazing, and it happens right here in St. Mary's in Ottawa.

A lot of hearts have been captured around St. Mary's Parish. I didn't capture any of them. I don't even know who half of them are. For example, a fellow I taught packed it in during his senior year in high school. He put everything on hold and walked away from the Lord. For eleven years, he didn't go to church, didn't pray. One day he ran into a former school chum of his having lunch at one of the local hospital cafes. The friend's heart had been captured years ago when he was in high school. The Lord still has his heart. He comes to St. Mary's once in awhile. The subject of church came up.

> The first fellow said: "I haven't been to church for eleven years."
> His buddy suggested: "Why don't you give St. Mary's a shot? It's not far from here. Remember Bedard? Big Bob? He's there."
> "Bedard! Really! Good heavens! I thought he was dead."
> "No! Almost, but he's still there."
> "Really? Well, maybe I'll check it out some day."

Came the inevitable day when he checked it out. He cried all through Mass. "I don't know what's happening to me," he told me later. I didn't either. I thought perhaps he was having some inner difficulty, maybe getting close to a nervous breakdown, but when we spoke later, I found out what was happening. I said, "The Lord is trying to catch your attention. He's touching your heart." So he proceeded to give his heart to the Lord. Today he is one of my right-hand men around here. That's the Lord's work. I can't do that. I didn't do it. God did. It happens again and again.

The first year that I came to St. Mary's, I went to a PTA meeting down at the school. As I circulated around I spotted a chap whom I had taught in grade nine. I remembered him as a pleasant young fellow.

> "Do you live around here," I asked?
> "Yes, just around the corner," he replied.
> "Oh really? Good," I countered. "We'll be seeing you."
> "I'm not into the church thing, though," he said. "Don't expect to see me there."
> I responded, "Ah well, that can always change." I didn't realize at the time how prophetic my words were.

It did change. Through a fairly typical process, the Lord caught this man's attention, captured his heart, and drew it to himself.

He set a fire in his soul that has transformed him completely. He's close to ten good years on the Lord's team at this writing.

3. To gather the disciples together

Jesus would go out on the road with his followers healing the sick and proclaiming the Good News. Then at night, he would gather the disciples together and teach them. The gospel writers sometimes say, "Jesus addressed the crowds." But at other times, they report, "Jesus said to the disciples." At other times, it's, "Jesus said to the apostles." He was saying different things to different groups, telling each what each needed to know.

Jesus called his disciples to a deeper commitment to him and to his ministry because he wanted to prepare them for the day when he wouldn't be around anymore. Then they would go out to the ends of the earth to do the things he had been doing for the house of Israel. These people became the Church. The Church was not a later development. The Church was founded by Jesus himself. If we allow the Lord to work fully in our lives, we become his disciples. We are then, the Church.

They returned from Capernaum and Jesus, once inside the house, began to ask them, "What were you discussing on the way home?" (Mark 9:33). This was the occasion on which they were talking about who was the greatest. He straightened them out. He taught them what it meant to be great, but he waited until he got them in the house to do that. He didn't embarrass them out on the road, in front of the crowds. That's a good example for all of us.

I am the vine, Jesus says, *and you are the branches* (John 15:5). St. Paul writes: The Father made Jesus head of the Church (*cf.* Eph 1:22). The Pope is not the head of the Church. Popes have never claimed that. In fact, they use the title 'Vicar of Christ'. Vicar means representative or deputy. Jesus is the head of his Church. A pastor is not really the head of a parish. He's actually Jesus' deputy. Jesus is head of the diocese. He's the Bishop. He's the pastor. He's the Pope. The rest of us are all simply his representatives. He's the head of our homes and our families. We are the stewards. Jesus is head of the Church. Let's make him head of our lives.

Peter became the rock upon which Jesus built the Church (*cf.* Matt 16:18). *Simon, do you love me?* (John 21:15), Jesus asked him three times. Each time Simon answered, "Yes." Jesus then bade him, *'Go and feed my lambs... tend my sheep... feed my sheep'* (John 21:15-17). Jesus was the Good Shepherd. He was going away and he was leaving another shepherd in his place—Simon Peter. We believe that is a specific reference to the Vicar of Christ, the Holy Father, the Pope.

Sometimes we Catholics are criticized for being a hierarchical Church. We'll get into that in detail in Chapter 4. For now, let's just notice how, from the disciples, who numbered in the hundreds, Jesus chose twelve, and called them 'Apostles.' Out of the twelve, he chose three—Peter, James and John—for specific things. Out of those three, he chose one—Peter, again—for a very specific role. Is there not a very clear hierarchical principle being established by Jesus himself while he was still on earth?

4. To go to the Cross

This was the Father's will and plan—that Jesus become the Paschal Lamb. He was offered up for our sins, for the salvation of the world.

The people of his day were not ready for Jesus as the sacrificial lamb. For them, if he was the Messiah, he had to be the fulfillment of the prophetic words in Daniel and other places that spoke of a conquering hero coming to wipe out, literally, all the Lord's enemies.

But there were other references in the Jewish Scriptures which spoke of a man of sorrow. Most of the theologians of Jesus' day would have said that these contrasting descriptions in their

Scriptures referred to two different people. The conqueror was the Messiah. The suffering servant was somebody else.

In reality, as Jesus has taught us, these contrasting sets of references refer, not to two people, but to one person who comes, not once, but twice. He has already come as the servant who suffered. He will come next as the conquering king. Actually, that's pretty exciting. I'm looking forward to it. Whether or not we have shuffled off this mortal coil in the meantime, we'll be part of it. We'll be witnesses to it. It will be a glorious day when Jesus comes in majesty, because every single human being who has ever lived on earth will be there to acknowledge him as Lord. There will be no room for dissent. Not everybody will like it, but they will all say it. They will have to, because there will not be room for any substitute for the truth.

Jesus was the suffering servant, fulfilling such prophecies as Psalm 22 which he recited on the Cross: *My God, my God, why have you forsaken me?* The psalm continues: "My body is racked. They are laughing at me. They are taking my garments and throwing dice for them" (*cf.* Ps 22:7, 14-15, 18). Amazing! It had been written 600 years before him, and, as he spoke it on the Cross, it was fulfilled right on the spot.

Will he be the one with no stately bearing, spurned and rejected?

> *A man of suffering, accustomed to infirmity...*
> *Yet it was our infirmities that he bore...*
> *While we thought of him as stricken,*
> *as one smitten by God and afflicted.*
> *But he was pierced for our offences...*
> *by his stripes we were healed...*
> *Though he was harshly treated, he submitted*
> *and opened not his mouth;*
> *Like a lamb led to the slaughter...*
> *he was silent and opened not his mouth.*

> *Oppressed and condemned, he was taken away...*
> *Though he had done no wrong.*
> *Through his suffering, my servant shall justify many...*
> *And he shall take away the sins of many,*
> *and win pardon for their offenses. (Isa 53:3-5, 7-9, 11-12)*

That's what Jesus was fulfilling as the suffering servant of whom Isaiah spoke. He came to do the will of his Father, and that meant going to the Cross.

Jesus purchased our salvation by dying on the Cross. He tied it in with the Paschal celebration, the Passover. That's the commemoration of the Lord's delivering of the Jews from Egypt. The Passover celebrated their freedom. During the final plague in Egypt, they marked the Lord's sign in blood on the doorposts of their houses, and they were passed over. Even now, it is one of the greatest celebrations of the year for the Jewish people. Jesus chose it to eat the Last Supper, as we call it, with his chosen band.

Every year at that time, the Jews gathered for the Paschal meal, and this time, as he celebrated it, Jesus himself was going to be the Lamb of sacrifice and go to the Cross the next day. On that evening, he gathered the Apostles around the table, took bread and wine, and celebrated what we now celebrate at the Eucharist. We are simply celebrating again the one sacrifice of Jesus of which he said: I have longed to have this meal with you. I have yearned for this night (*cf.* Luke 22:15). It's not another sacrifice. People who don't understand it think we are multiplying sacrifices. Actually we're not. We are just doing what Jesus has told us to do. We're simply making his sacrifice present again and again.

Jesus went to the Cross and became the Paschal Lamb. His Blood is sufficient reparation and atonement for our sins. Because he became one of us, we benefit. *You who once were far off have been brought near through the blood of Christ* (Eph 2:13).

He cancelled the bond that stood against us with all its claims, snatching it up and nailing it to the cross (Col 2:14). He is the *one mediator between God and men* (1 Tim 2:5).

Death looks like our final enemy, the end of the road, but it has never been God's idea. *God did not make death* (Wis 1:13). God's offer is life—life to the full—but we have chosen otherwise. We have contrived death ourselves. Nevertheless, Jesus has defeated that enemy through the Cross. Once Jesus gave up his life and breathed out his last, the new covenant was in place.

5. To send the Holy Spirit

Who is the Holy Spirit, and what does he mean to us? We'll get quickly to that. That's the topic of the next chapter.

To sum up, Jesus is the narrow gate, the one way to the Father, the only name by which we may be saved. We need to surrender to him. We need to come to terms with him, to give our whole lives to him.

As one person put it a few years ago: "Once Jesus is perceived for who he is, only one response makes any sense at all, and that's total. Anything else is insane." There's a lot of truth in that. To him we surrender everything. It's the best move we can ever make. I can testify to that myself. The best thing I've ever done was turn my life over to Jesus Christ. I've probably done a few other things that were reasonably good. I coached teams to some basketball championships—that was pretty good. I taught Canadian history to a lot of people, some of whom wound up liking it—that was pretty good, too. I talked my head off in almost every place in Canada—and that was okay as well. But the best thing I've ever done is turn my life over to the Lord. That makes me his disciple. The Church—you and I—is meant to be the gathering together of those who have made that choice and are trying to live discipleship out on a daily basis. We have to start somewhere. Sooner or later we have to come to terms with Jesus Christ.

The good majority of students in my classes were not at all sure that God was real. I would tell them: "If you don't think God is real, or if you are not sure, tell him, 'Lord, if you're real, show me. I give you the green light.'" To those who surrendered their lives to him he revealed himself. It was amazing. It continues to be my greatest delight.

There's just nothing quite like seeing God touch and capture hearts.

Study Questions:

1 Fr. Bob quotes many scriptures describing who Jesus is and what he accomplished. Which ones most deeply impact you and why?

2 Why was it the Father's will that Jesus go to the Cross as part of his five-fold mission in the world?

3 Fr. Bob says, "Once Jesus is perceived for who he is, only one response makes any sense at all, and that's total. Anything else is insane... To him we surrender everything. It's the best move we can ever make."

We invite you to reflect upon and pray the following prayer used by Fr. Bob:

Jesus, I want you to be the Lord of my life in every possible way. I give you my understanding, my will, my spirit, my physical being, my possessions, my desires and my plans. I want to surrender to you completely. I choose you as my Lord and Saviour. Help me to know you not only as Master, Redeemer, and King but also my friend. I give you my cares, my worries, my fears, my hang-ups, all my difficulties, and I ask you to set me free. Amen.

CHAPTER THREE

The Holy Spirit

In the previous chapter, I was trying to make the point that what the Father wants for us first of all is to surrender to Jesus. The question for each of us in this chapter is: "Have I surrendered yet?"

Maybe some people are saying, "I've been in the Church all these years, but I'm not familiar with this word 'surrender'." Fair enough. Then how about the good old Catholic word "consecration"? Have I consecrated my life to the Saviour yet? That's the question.

I start by surrendering to Jesus himself. Next I get empowered by the Holy Spirit. I put my roots down in the Church that Jesus has founded. I come under authority within the Church. Only then can I work for God, and not before.

Jesus, along with the Father, has sent the Holy Spirit. John the Baptist says that Jesus will baptize us with the Holy Spirit (Matt 3:11, Mark 1:8, Luke 3:16, and John 1:33). There are very few things which are common to all four Gospels, but the baptism with the Holy Spirit is one of them.

The first three Gospels, called the "Synoptic Gospels", have a lot of things in common. The Gospel of St. John is like a complement to the other three, and repeats very few things that the other three have written. One of the few is this reference to being baptized with the Holy Spirit:

> *The one who sent me to baptize with water told me, 'When you see the Spirit descend and rest on someone, it is he who is to baptize with the Holy Spirit.' Now I have seen for my self and have testified, 'This is God's chosen One.'* (John 1:33-34)

In other words, John is saying: Don't put me on a pedestal. Another one is coming. I'm his herald. I have baptized you with water, but when he gets here, he will baptize you with the Holy Spirit. These words were spoken right at the very beginning of Jesus' public ministry. He had just left his home in Nazareth. He had bidden goodbye to his mother and the ones called his brothers and sisters (I suspect they were children of his uncle who had died), and he had gone to meet John who was baptizing in the Jordan.

Jesus had a fair bit to say about the Holy Spirit. When he was just about to go back to his Father, he said: *Wait in the city. Do not leave Jerusalem, because the Father's promise is about to be fulfilled. Not many days from now you will all be baptized with the Holy Spirit* (Acts 1:4-5 paraphrase). The promise of the Father was the coming of the Holy Spirit.

Jesus left his followers with a sense of anticipation. He wanted them to have an air of expectancy about the arrival of the Holy Spirit.

What was the Holy Spirit going to do? *When the Holy Spirit comes upon you,* Jesus says, *you will receive power. Then you will be my witnesses not only in Jerusalem, but throughout Judea and Samaria, and indeed to the ends of the earth* (Acts 1:8 JB). In other words: you will receive power from the Holy Spirit and, if you surrender to that power properly, get rooted in the Church, and become one in mind and heart, the Holy Spirit will give power to your witness. We are called to be witnesses of Jesus but our witness is not going to have much power if it is just ours. If the Holy Spirit is in it, it's going to have power to effect what God wants, namely, the conversion of somebody else. That's what witnessing is for.

The Holy Spirit will give us power. What the Father wants is what Jesus has proclaimed and what the Holy Spirit will make possible. The role of the Holy Spirit is to make possible the work of God. We don't have to operate under our own steam. One of the problems with us as members of the Church is that we try too hard. It does not depend on how hard we work. It depends on how surrendered we are to God and how the Holy Spirit can work through us. It doesn't have to exhaust us. We are not supposed to get burnt out trying to do the work of God. The Holy Spirit is supposed to do the firing and the burning.

It isn't human effort we need. It is human decision, human permission, and human surrender. If we come together as the body of Christ and nothing really happens, it's because the Holy Spirit is not stirred up in the body of believers. It's the Holy Spirit's role, then, to get things going.

Jesus says *I have come to bring fire to the earth, and how I wish it were blazing already* (Luke 12:49 JB). The fire is the Holy Spirit.

Jesus, in other words, is saying: "I am eager to send you the Holy Spirit, but I have things to accomplish first. I must go to all the towns of Israel to proclaim the Good News, to touch and heal the sick, to call the Church together. Then I have to go to the Cross. But after all that is finished, I will send the Holy Spirit. How I long, he says, for that day to come."

In my day there was no kindergarten. We started in grade one—'Baby Class' as we called it. I can still see page one of our catechism:

> Q: "Why did God make us?"
>
> A: "To know, to love and to serve him here on this earth, and to be happy with him forever in the next."

This is our destiny. The Holy Spirit will draw us more deeply into the life of God. St. Augustine put it as well as anybody ever has: "You have made us for yourself, O Lord, and our hearts are restless, until they rest in you." What a profound mystery! The world doesn't know it. We are so busy doing so many things. This life is a mere snap of the fingers compared to the eternity we will spend with God. In high school, students would sometimes say: "Heaven sounds so dull. I don't want to sit around playing a harp." That is not what it will be like. Heaven will be a place of breathless activity, and our destiny is to be swept up into it.

St. Paul writes: He has anointed and sealed us (*cf.* 2 Cor 1:22), referring to the Holy Spirit, the first payment.

The Holy Spirit testifies to Jesus: *When the Paraclete comes*, Jesus says, *the Spirit of Truth who comes from the Father, and whom I myself will send from the Father, he will bear witness on my behalf* (John 15:26). Together the Father and Jesus send the Holy Spirit, and the latter, in obedience, comes. The Holy Spirit is just as obedient and submitted to the Father's will as Jesus was and is. A Paraclete is one who is called to the side of another in need of assistance. The Holy Spirit will help us, will get involved with us, will work with us and through us, and stay with us. When this Paraclete comes, Jesus would say, he will bear witness on my behalf. If you allow me to baptize you with the Holy Spirit, you will have no question about who I am. Once the Holy Spirit witnesses to you, you'll know who I am—The Word of God, the one sent from the Father, true God from true God.

I was on a retreat one time where the retreat master referred to a theological question being studied in a lot of our institutions:

Who really is Jesus? The preacher said: "If you want to know who Jesus is, surrender to the Holy Spirit." He will bear witness on Jesus' behalf. The Holy Spirit proceeds from the Father and the Son. That's in the Nicene Creed. The Holy Spirit will interact with my spirit to reveal to me who Jesus is, and then I can begin to know him as a living person. It's a spiritual thing. I can't put it in a test tube. I can't chart it out on a blackboard. I can't write it all up in a book. It's something that happens in my own spirit.

There was a nun who was asked one time on a television program: "Sister, how do you know who this Jesus is?" "I know it in my knower," she said. How can we get into an intellectual discussion with a person like that?

> "I know because I know, you see."
> "How do you know?"
> "I just know."
> "Oh. Could I come to know, too?"
> "Of course you can."
> "How do I do it?"
> "Surrender. That's the key."

When I am baptized with the Holy Spirit, I experience a spiritual awakening. It is as though I have received a new pair of eyes to see what God is doing in the world, and a new pair of ears to hear his Word.

When I hear God's Word, I recognize it if the Holy Spirit is working within me. It's a spiritual matter. It operates at the level of the human spirit. We are not just bodies; we are also spirit made in the image and likeness of God. We know that, but a lot of people fight it. They want proof. "Show us," they'll say.

The Holy Spirit deals in truth and stays with us. Jesus says, *I will ask the Father and he will give you another* [*Advocate*] *to be with you always: the Spirit of Truth, whom the world cannot accept, since it neither sees him nor recognizes him* (John 14:16-17). If I do not surrender myself to God, I will never know him. The Holy

Spirit cannot work through me. All I can see is what I see.

One of the good things about coaching high school basketball was winning. The other good thing about it was that the Lord would sometimes catch the attention of some of the young athletes, and they would start to pray. They would become baptized with the Holy Spirit and get enthused about the Lord.

I remember one young man, though, that I coached, who didn't come along that way. He was a fine athlete and a fine chap, but he didn't believe in God. In fact he had never been baptized. He said, "I believe what I see. I cannot believe what I cannot see." That's fair enough, but we'll never see the Lord until we come before him in surrender and open up our hearts to him.

Jesus said, *I am with you always, until the end of the world* (Matt 28:20). What did his words mean? He is with us in the Eucharist—true. But it's the Holy Spirit who brings Jesus to life in our hearts and souls. It's through the Holy Spirit that Jesus fulfills his promise to be with us. The world believes only what it sees. 'Prove it', the world says. The inner reality of God is perceived only by those who surrender to him. The world can never accomplish that. It doesn't come through argument, or reasoning, or bargaining, or being worthy, but rather through surrender of the whole person. If I am created by God, then I am in total subjection to him. He's made me free. Jesus was free, but he always chose the will of his Father. If we could imitate him, then we would know God. If we freely surrender whatever we are—body, mind, will, heart, soul, spirit—then the Lord can come to us and live within us.

Coming to that point of surrender can be a big struggle for a lot of people. And for many, the more intelligent they are, the more difficult they find it to surrender. People of high intellectual capacity tend naturally to feel they should be able to figure everything out. But God can't be figured out. We don't reason our way to God. We surrender our way to him.

One of the brightest students I ever taught was having doubts about his faith. When I reminded him he had always learned everything easily, he agreed. "Yes," he said. "I've always been able to figure everything out." I told him God was too big to fit into his head. The route he needed was surrender.

What makes us think that we can understand all reality? What makes us think that there is nothing that transcends us? I don't know the answer to that, but a lot of people would say: "Unless you can convince me, I will not believe." I am not out to convince anybody. Teaching within the Church is not so much to convince people of things, but rather to exhort them to come in surrender to God and to allow him to reveal himself to them.

I used to say to my senior religion class: "Look, if you're not sure about God, give him a chance. Say: 'Lord, if you're real, show me.'"

One of the girls came to see me about it and told me she didn't believe in God at all. Then she told me why. It was a sad story. She had been into everything. She had hit the streets when she was twelve. She'd been involved in promiscuity and alcohol and drugs. She had attempted suicide three times before she was sixteen. But then at sixteen she began to straighten out her life. It was her parents who made it possible.

I'll never forget what she said:

> "My parents never turned their backs on me. No matter what shape I was in, they always took me back. With their help, I eventually cleaned up my life. But I don't believe in God. I can't believe in any God who would allow a little girl to go through the hell that I went through."
>
> "There aren't any real good reasons not to believe in God," I replied, "but you've got the best of the poor ones. I can understand how you feel. But why don't you

> give him a chance? Say, 'Lord, if you're real, show me.'"
>
> "But if I don't believe he's there," she said, "how can I talk to him?"
>
> "But maybe he is there." I responded, "What have you got to lose? Go ahead and try it anyway. I won't tell anybody."

Eventually she did try it. And the Lord did reveal himself to her. I got a note from her about two months after the school year ended thanking me for what I had done and saying that, although she still had a long way to go, she felt she had developed the same kind of faith as I had. Tears came to my eyes as I read it. "Hey, Lord," I said, "you came through again!" The Lord always comes through.

Another young fellow, Steve by name, came in to discuss a problem. I was used to hearing problems from students.

> "Father," he said, "I'm worried about something."
> "Yes, Steve. What is it?"
> "It's my sister. She's in a relationship that's really bad. I'm really concerned."

I was edified that he was concerned about his sister.

> "I tried to talk to her," he continued, "but she told me to mind my business. Then I tried to talk to the guy she's involved with and he threatened to punch me out. So I've been praying. I haven't seen God do anything about it yet, but I have the impression that he is going to do something about it soon."

How about that for an eighteen-year-old?

> "Well, Steve," I said, "that sounds like a pretty strong faith you've got going there."
> "Yes. I guess you could say that, Father."
> "Steve," I replied, "did you always have this kind of faith?"
> "No, not really, Father. In fact in grade eleven I quit

> altogether. I packed it in. I stopped going to church. Stopped praying. I figured the whole thing was just fantasy. I wasn't going to bother with that stuff anymore. I stayed in school here because my friends were here and it's a good school. But I was listening in Religion class at the beginning of the year and I heard you say that if we weren't sure about God, to give him a chance and to say: 'Lord, if you're real, show me.' So I started to say that every night before I went to bed. He showed me. Now I know."

It was as simple as that. How did he know? He just knew it inside. I don't imagine he would have given any great impressive testimony about it, but that's the way God works. The boy's life was changed.

He went on to finish high school and went into carpentry. Each year for the next three years, almost on the day of the anniversary of our talk, I would run into him here and there. He was still a changed man. Isn't it amazing how God works?

The Paraclete, the Holy Spirit whom the Father will send in my name, will instruct you in everything, and remind you of all that I told you, says Jesus (John 14:26). The Holy Spirit is the principal teacher. I saw that again and again in school. I hate to use so many examples from school, but believe that, if God can work with people sixteen, seventeen and eighteen, he can work with anybody. They have, as they see it, their whole lives before them with options of all kinds. In some ways, the world is at their doorstep. But also, they're faced with all the enticements of the world. There's great pressure on them to conform to the world's ways. If God can deal with them, he can deal with anybody.

One sixteen-year-old in grade eleven had just gone through a whole spiritual awakening, including being baptized with the Holy Spirit. Two weeks later he was talking to me about the Prophet Isaiah, discussing the meaning of chapter 47, verse 2.

He still had lots to learn, but his grasp was impressive. I said, "Where did you learn all this stuff? How long have you been studying it?" "I just started to read this a couple of weeks ago," he said.

How did he do it? The Holy Spirit is the teacher. We have the official teachings of the Church and lots of us within the Church are supposed to teach, but the Holy Spirit is the main teacher.

Jesus says, *I have much more to tell you, but you cannot bear it now. When he comes, however, being the Spirit of truth he will guide you to all truth...* (John 16:12-13). It probably won't happen all at once, but happen it will. Jesus didn't teach everything. He didn't meet every need, or address every situation. He left that to the Church and to the Holy Spirit. And one of the things the Holy Spirit would do is teach the Church. Jesus founded the Church and sent the Holy Spirit to guide it.

Chapters 13:31 through 17:27 of the Gospel of St. John are usually called Jesus' 'Last Discourse'. He is speaking at the Last Supper to the Apostles—to the leaders of the Church. He is telling them that the Holy Spirit is essential. *It is much better for you that I go* [because,] *if I fail to go, the Paraclete will never come to you* (John 16:7). Those who heard him could not understand that. They might have been saying something like: "What do you mean it's better for you to go? It's better for you to stay. Stay for heaven's sake! We'd be lost without you." And Jesus would say, "No, you won't. In fact, it will be better if I go." This is the Father's plan, and unlikely as it seemed to them, Jesus had to leave and it was better that he did so. The Spirit's coming coincided with Jesus' going and was necessarily involved with the beginning of the Church.

Jesus built up an expectation about the Holy Spirit and then he ascended to the Father. *Remain here in the city,* he said to his followers, *until you are clothed with power from on high* (Luke 24:49). Ten days later the big day arrived. They were gathered in the upper room and they were praying. There probably were

120 or so of them, including the Apostles, a number of disciples, Mary, Jesus' mother, and the men who were called his brothers—James, Joseph, Simon and Jude. The Holy Spirit had come many times in the past to perform specific tasks, like operating through Moses to lead the people out of slavery in Egypt. This time was different. The Holy Spirit was coming to stay and to give power to the works that God himself had ordained. The Father would ordain the work. The Holy Spirit would give the power.

It's all documented in the second chapter of the Acts of the Apostles. In verse 2, there is a noise like a rushing wind and the walls are beginning to vibrate. In verse 3, fire appears over their heads. Jesus had said: *I have come to bring fire to the earth, and how I wish it were blazing already* (Luke 12:49 JB). This is the fire. It is a sign of the Holy Spirit's presence. In verse 4, they are given tongues to proclaim God's Word—a gift specifically for this day so that they could go out and speak the Good News in their own language and those who heard them would hear it in theirs. It was a fair-sized miracle.

In verse 6, they go out into the public square where a large crowd has gathered. The crowd is made up of all kinds of people—Jews mostly—from all over the world. At that time, there were more Jews living outside Palestine than inside. Some of them would make a pilgrimage to the Temple in Jerusalem for the feasts of Passover, Pentecost and Tabernacles. There were people in the city from every nation, each speaking his or her own language. The disciples of Jesus are very enthused and speaking with great conviction. The skeptical ones in the crowd say: "What's the matter with them? The way they're carrying on, they must be drunk" (*cf.* Acts 2:12-13).

Then Peter gets up to speak. He is the obvious spokesman. He's the one whom Jesus had taken aside and said three times, *"Peter do you love me? Be the shepherd. Feed my sheep"* (John 21:17 paraphrase). Jesus, the Good Shepherd, was going away and he was leaving another shepherd in his place. Peter, the first father after Pentecost to God's people, the Church, would go on to explain: "We are not drunk. We're not coming from a party. It's only nine o'clock in the morning. This is something you don't understand, but let me explain it to you" (*cf.* Acts 2:14-15). He goes on to talk about the fulfilment of the prophecy of Joel. *In the last days there will be prophecy, visions, dreams* (Joel 2:28 paraphrase). In other words, the Holy Spirit will move this body of people in ways they are not used to.

Are we open to things like that today? Visions? Dreams? Prophetic utterances? We have to be. These gifts are vital for the Church and yet, at the same time, it's a hazardous field, because the minute we tell people God is ready to speak, there are a hundred people knocking on the door saying that God has spoken to them. It's exhausting, but it's important. All must be discerned with some care.

Peter would go on to say: "Jesus is the long-awaited one. He is the one for whom we have been waiting, the one the prophets have spoken of, the one the psalmists have referred to. He's the one" (*cf.* Acts 2:25-36). A lot of people in the crowd were shaken by Peter's words. They *were cut to the heart* and some said, *What must we do?* (Acts 2:37). The Holy Spirit was at work in their hearts. Peter urged them to repent, to get out of sin, to be baptized, to come into the body of believers and to receive the Holy Spirit.

Right away the Church began to grow and to respond. As long as the Church responds to the Holy Spirit, he will give the growth. In God's plan, the Church is not meant to decline, is not meant to stagnate, is not meant to hold the line. It is meant to grow.

The early Church was faithful to four things:
the teaching of the Apostles;
the shared life;
the breaking of the bread;
the common prayers (*cf.* Acts 2:42).

The Holy Spirit came that first Pentecost, fifty days after the resurrection of Jesus, and has never left. This may come as a surprise to some, but the Holy Spirit did not make his debut among us thirty years ago. The Holy Spirit has been here right from the beginning, doing the work of the Father whenever God's people have allowed him to do so.

The New Testament enumerates some thirty different spiritual gifts. Some of them are built upon natural talents, but others are not. What God wants is that we yield to his plan. How do we find out what it is? We have just to tell him we'll take on anything he wants us to. He'll get through to us.

Here's a listing of the gifts in no particular order: prophecy, service, teaching, exhortation, almsgiving, leadership, mercy, wisdom, knowledge, faith, healing, miracles, discerning spirits, tongues, interpretation of tongues, being an apostle, administration, evangelizing, pastoring, celibacy, voluntary poverty, hospitality, being a missionary, music, preaching, writing, intercession, exorcism, deliverance, martyrdom.

These are all gifts of the Holy Spirit. What good shape the Church would be in if they were all fully operational!

What we are talking about here are authentic religious experiences, but we have to bear in mind that there can be all kinds of spurious, phoney experiences as well. It is not a simple matter. Sometimes spiritual things can spill over into the emotions. Everything has to be very carefully discerned. It's a realm we're not comfortable with because we are not yet finished with the so-called Age of Enlightenment. We have become an overly cerebral Church. We have forgotten, to a large extent, the experiential dimension of faith. Why do people stop going to church? I'm convinced it's because they're short on authentic spiritual experience.

People who are familiar with genuine religious experience don't ordinarily quit going to church. Evangelicals and Pentecostals use the handy phrase 'born again'. Actually, it's not a bad way to describe the experience. My problem with it is that it seems to imply a one-time unrepeatable grace. I would prefer something like 'spiritual awakening', something that can occur several times.

In any case, it is an unmistakable touch from God. And it works to change the person who receives it. Conversation changes. Perspectives change. Priorities change. People begin to hunger for God's Word. They get enthused about serving him. They discover an intense desire to share their experience. They want to get rooted in the Church. And, if they continue to respond to the promptings of the Holy Spirit, they will want to become socially involved as well.

A number of Protestant denominations speak of being 'saved'. A typical member could tell us the day and hour when he/she was saved. Or born again. It is the same reality that Catholics understand as the state of grace. If I am in the state of grace, the state of friendship with God, am I saved? Of course I am. Can I lose it? I certainly can. Some people in other faiths call it 'backsliding'. I remember being driven to the airport a few years ago. My driver talked about his eighteen year old son.

"How does your son stand with the Lord," I asked. "He is saved, but backslidden," he replied. I understood exactly what he meant. He meant that the Lord had touched his life, but that he had fallen away again. He was back to his old ways. As Catholics, we would say he's turned his back on the Lord. He's living in sin, or at least, it would seem so from outward appearances.

Religious experiences are gifts from God. For many people, they are the introduction to knowing the Lord himself.

I know a young fellow who came from a good family, but, for him, his religion was a matter of external observance. He played the game. He went to church with his parents because he knew that if he didn't, they'd give him a very hard time. So he went.

But it didn't mean much to him. He was simply waiting for the time when he could opt out like everybody else. But when he was seventeen, he got down on his knees and surrendered his life to the Lord.

He later said to me: "Father, the day I surrendered my life to the Lord, it was like waking up after being asleep for seventeen years." This young man is now thirty-five years old or so and he's on the parish council at his church. The fire is still burning. We can call it what we want—the touch of God, Baptism with the Holy Spirit, spiritual awakening—but that's the way it works.

The Holy Spirit is not an afterthought. The Holy Spirit is not a prize for the pious. The Holy Spirit is not an option for those who are interested. Without the Holy Spirit, the hearts of believers would grow cold. We would become God's frozen people. Without the Holy Spirit, the Church would become the Catholic Historical Society instead of the Church of the Living God. We are supposed to be a body that is moving and alive.

We underestimate God's desire and his capacity to relate directly to us. Have we ever heard it said that we can only contact God through other people? I've heard that within the Church. Baloney! Of course we can contact God through other people, but we can be in touch with God directly as well. He is present not only in his people but he is transcendent as well. He exists quite apart from his creation.

A final question for this chapter: "Have we been baptized with the Holy Spirit?" We have certainly received the Holy Spirit if we have been baptized, but we don't have the experience until we make a conscious surrender to the Lord.

The Holy Spirit, if we will let him, will provide us with whatever we need to enter into the kind of relationship with God that God wants for us.

I was ordained twenty years before I experienced being baptized with the Holy Spirit. I had been, at the time, seventeen years involved in high school work. I was honest, I think. I worked hard at what seemed like God's work for me. I was decent. I don't believe I scandalized anybody. I had become a good teacher. And a good basketball coach. I think I helped a few of the students to become better persons.

But I had given up praying. I just couldn't do it. I had no skill and no real taste for it. I kidded myself that my work was my prayer.

Came then an opportunity to open up to the transforming work of the Holy Spirit. It was a Life in the Spirit seminar. I was one of a group of a dozen or so 'candidates'. The leader urged us to ask specifically for some of the Corinthian gifts, the charisms of the Holy Spirit—things like prophecy, miracles, and tongues.

I wasn't really sure what I thought of those things. I remember saying to the Lord something like: "If you don't want to give me any of those gifts they're talking about, that's OK. But there is one thing I want, something I desperately need. I need a gift of prayer. Can you give me that?" I actually didn't know if there was such a thing as a gift of prayer. But I knew that was what I needed.

When the night arrived that we were to invoke the action of the Holy Spirit, I asked for my gift of prayer. I surrendered to Jesus as the Lord and Saviour of my life and asked him to baptize me with the Holy Spirit.

It was a very low-key experience. There were no fireworks, but there was lots of peace. And my request was granted. I asked for a gift of prayer. Within twenty-four hours I was praying up a storm. I couldn't get enough of it. And not only did I now want to pray. I was good at it. What a blessing! That's the work of the Holy Spirit.

The gift of the Holy Spirit is available to all. Is there a process? Actually there is. I begin by repenting of my sins. A good Confession would be highly recommended. I then surrender my life to Jesus as Lord and Saviour and invite him to take over. I finish by asking him to baptize me with the Holy Spirit. That should do it.

I have to realize that God, my loving Father, wants to give me every good blessing, including and especially his Spirit. The Father never refuses the Holy Spirit to those who ask (*cf.* Luke 11:13).

Study Questions:

1 What promises does the Father make about the coming of the Holy Spirit?

2 Fr. Bob shares some powerful stories of surrender to the Lord in this chapter. Do you feel that you have given full freedom to the Holy Spirit in your life? Explain.

3 Fr. Bob says, "The gift of the Holy Spirit in available to all. Is there a process? Actually there is. I begin by repenting of my sins. A good confession would be highly recommended. I then surrender my life to Jesus as Lord and Savior and invite him to take over. I finish by asking him to baptize me with the Holy Spirit."

We invite you to pray the following prayer:

Loving Father, thank you for the gift of life. Thank you for preparing a place for me, a place for all of us in your Kingdom. Thank you for sending your Son Jesus to become one of us. Lord Jesus, thank you for your saving action, for your death and resurrection, which has opened the gates of life. The Father has made you Lord and King. I choose you now as my Lord and King. You have said that you would baptize us with the Holy Spirit. I desire this and ask you for it now. Baptize me with your Holy Spirit. Plant me firmly in the Church and use me as you wish. Amen.

CHAPTER FOUR

The Church

God's inspired Word makes it clear that he has a preference for peoplehood. God wants to call people together in relationship to one another, as well as to him. That was the case in Old Testament times with the Jewish nation and it is the case with the Church now. Today, we are God's people, if we will allow ourselves to be. We, the Church, are the new Israel growing out of the Israel of old.

God himself is family. The Father, Son and Holy Spirit are persons in relationship. We imitate him in relationship to one another. It is made clear in New Testament writings that we are designed to function as a body with many parts. God has made us all different.

The Church is not our idea. We don't have to apologize for it. Jesus founded the Church because the Father led him to do so. In obedience to the Father, he called the Church together. We mess it up, of course, but he continually wants to renew it and revive it. We are imperfect. He is perfect.

The theme of Vatican II was the renewal of the Church. Pope

John XXIII's theme for it was *Ecclesia semper reformanda*—"the Church stands always in need of reform." Why? Because it has human beings in it who need renewal and revival. God is always looking for people who are available to him so that he can renew and revive the Church through them. This is the 'remnant' the Bible speaks of again and again.

It is our task to bring people to Jesus. This is the first conversion. Then he takes over and brings them to the Church—the second conversion. The Church is divine because Jesus founded it. It is his idea, his will, his program. Because it is divine, it is holy. In every year of the Church's history there have been distinct marks of holiness within it. The Church is also human because we're it. As Vatican II pointed out clearly, we are the people of God. But because it is human, it is sinful. Right from the start there have been problems within the Church, and lots of disedifying things have taken place down through its history. There are lots of disedifying things still happening in the Church now. Why? Because the Church is human.

The Church is human and people get hurt in it. Have we been hurt within the Church? Have we ever met anybody who is still so hurt by what happened within the Church that he/she has never gone back? It happens. Why? Because the Church is made up of sinful people and we can hurt one another. What are we supposed to do for people that are hurt? Love them, minister to them in whatever way we can and be gentle with them. We can say, "You are welcome. Come back anytime. Don't blame God for the things that have happened to you. It wasn't his idea. If you want to be forgiven of any of your sins, you have to forgive, and that includes forgiving the Church as well."

The fact that the Church is sinful and human is no reason for abandoning it. Knocking the Church and digging up scandals is totally unproductive. It goes absolutely nowhere. Yet some people devote the better part of a lifetime to such pursuit. The Crusades and the Inquisition happened. Why? Because the

Church was human and sinful. People did those things, not God.

It's easier to be critical than to get involved, isn't it? When I was a teacher, I used to say school would be a fantastic place if it weren't for the students. The Church would be an incredible place to be if it weren't for the people. That's human nature. We have to love the Church. We have to get involved with it, whether we like it or not. The work of the Kingdom is to be done by the Church.

Note that the Church is not the same thing as the Kingdom of God. The Kingdom of God is the fullness of the Father's will. The role of the Church is to call people to become part of the Kingdom of God. The poet Wordsworth never went to church. He used to walk in the woods and commune with God. That's a good thing to do, but it's easier to do that than it is to get involved with people. Relationships are always threatening. The Church involves relationships, not only with God, but with one another under God.

God calls for us to love the Church with all its spots, wrinkles and barnacles. Do we love the Church? The Lord wants us to. If we have problems with that, we might want to consider asking him for the gift to love his Church.

The Lord wants us to be effective ministers of the Kingdom, but our 'ineffectiveness quotient' is in direct proportion to our resistance to his Word. We are a rebellious people. We like to do things our own way. Don't we like to have our meals when we want them? Don't we like to eat the things that we want to eat? Don't we want to schedule our day the way we want to run it? Of course we do! But don't we realize that is the root of sin? God has a plan, but our willfulness gets in his way. We have no power of our own, but how powerful God would be able to work through us, if only we could be fully submitted to his Word.

Forming the Church was the third of the five major things that Jesus came to do—the first being to proclaim the Good News, the second to do the works of God (such as healing the sick), and the third thing was to call the Church together. Jesus called people after him. He taught them. He prepared them. He lived with them. He corrected them. He encouraged them. The fourth thing he did was go to the Cross. And then he ascended into heaven—but not before he placed others in charge. The fifth thing he did was, with his Father, send the Holy Spirit.

The earliest chronicles of the Church in action are presented by St. Luke in the Acts of the Apostles. These are preserved for us in God's plan because we have lessons to learn from the Word of God, particularly about how the Church began and the way it grew into what it is today.

Once the immediate Pentecost experience was over, the Church began to grow. The first ten verses of Acts 3 tell the story of how Peter and John cured a crippled man. Peter said: *Silver and gold, I have none, but what I have, I give you: In the name of Jesus Christ of Nazareth, arise and walk* (Acts 3:6 Douay). And he got up, he walked, and he ran! Right away, the Church experienced the power of God in the healing of a crippled man.

As the Church of God today, we are meant to experience his power in the same way. If we are not experiencing it, then we have to search into the mind of God as to why we are not. I would suggest the reason is a resistance in some way to his Word.

The Lord wants us to be one people. He asks us to be of one mind and one heart (*cf.* Eph 4:3). If there is anybody who is resisting God's call to be one body, then our work as a body is going to be compromised and ineffective to that degree. Again, our ineffectiveness quotient is in direct proportion to our resistance to the Word of God.

God has done something that needs an explanation. Peter is the one whom Jesus has left with a special role as leader. Peter is the logical spokesman. He tells them it was not the Apostles' power that healed the cripple. It was the power of God. He proclaims Jesus, and calls people to submit to him as Lord and Saviour. Proclaiming Jesus must also be our number one role as a Church. That's why, when I first came to St. Mary's, I thought it a good thing to print at the bottom of the bulletin: "St. Mary's Church is a Catholic parish proclaiming Jesus Christ as Lord and King." Not that other parishes weren't doing the same thing, but I wanted to give that a special emphasis. "Jesus is Lord" has to be our first proclamation of the Gospel.

Peter and John get arrested for causing a public disturbance (Acts 4:1-4).

They had performed works of power. They proclaimed it. They explained it and they were harassed. We are going to be harassed too. We can expect to be criticized, put down, made fun of. Have we ever been criticized for proclaiming the fullness of the Gospel of Christ? It's probably a good sign if we have. We can all expect to be harassed in one way or other if we stand up for the Gospel of Christ. We don't have to go looking for it. If we are faithful to living out the Gospel, it will come to us. If we aren't getting criticized, it probably means we're not doing much to promote the Lord's Gospel.

When Mary and Joseph brought the infant Jesus to the temple for presentation, the prophet Simeon said that the child would be a sign of contradiction. We become the same thing when we stand up for the Gospel of Christ.

Having been arrested, Peter and John are called up before the Sanhedrin, the highest religious legislative body in Israel. Once again Peter speaks to them very clearly: "We will proclaim the name of Jesus until the day we die because there is no salvation in any other name" (*cf.* Acts 4:12-20). Our message has to be the same. We have to show a sensitivity about it, but we have to be clear.

The Sanhedrin decides to warn them. "Don't do this again,"

they say. "We have had enough of this. Don't ever mention his name around town again. We don't want rumours spreading about this empty tomb. You get out there and be quiet." The Apostles get released, but they are anything but quiet.

In Acts 4:23-31, Luke describes a meeting of the faithful. At this meeting of believers, here is how they prayed: *"Grant to your servants, even as they speak your words, complete assurance by stretching forth your hand in cures and signs and wonders to be worked in the name of Jesus"* (Acts 4:29). We have to be a people who will ask regularly for the Lord to stretch out his hand in power and do his work so that people's attention will be caught and they can come to believe.

While the disciples are praying, the walls shake and they are deeply touched by the Holy Spirit. Having been through the Pentecost experience once already, they go through it again. Would we say that the Church at that time was dull, lifeless and drab, and that what they did was mechanical, routine and dead? Not even close! Their gatherings were alive, and our celebrations are meant to be the same. When people come to take part in our liturgies, they are supposed to experience life. They are supposed to sense a presence of God. When they leave, they should be able to say, "Something's happening in that church. I don't know what it is, but something is definitely happening." Church is not entertainment, but it's not supposed to be lifeless either. It certainly wasn't then.

Ananias and Sapphira (*cf.* Acts 5), are the less than wholehearted disciples, who scheme to keep a portion for themselves in spite of the fact that everybody else is giving all. They renege on their commitment and they both die suddenly when confronted with the truth. Did God strike them dead? I don't think so. I think they were just confronted with the enormity of what they had done. They had betrayed their commitment, and out they went. So right away, there are problems. This was the first sign that Scriptures give us of internal difficulties in the Church.

Have we got problems in the Church today? Of course we have. Do we have some people going one way and others going another? Surely, we do. Even now, things aren't much different. But that's not the Holy Spirit's work. That's the human factor.

Signs keep occurring. More signs. More power. People bring the sick out on stretchers and lay them in the street in the hope that even the shadow of Peter (*cf.* Acts 5:15) will fall upon them as he goes by and they will be healed. Now that's power!

Then there is a second arrest. This time all the Apostles are put in jail. However, they are delivered from prison miraculously. An angel comes and opens the gates and says, "That's it, men. Out you go. The Lord doesn't want you in prison. There are things to do." Back they go to the temple square to do their work again. Can we see how the verses of the Acts of the Apostles are fairly crackling with the power of God? This is to be our experience too.

They are arrested a third time. They are brought up before the Sanhedrin again. The members of the Sanhedrin are furious, outraged. How dare these upstarts do the thing they are told not to do? How dare they cure the sick? One of the members of the Sanhedrin, a chap by the name of Gamaliel, probably the most famous teacher of the law in those days and the one under whom the Apostle Paul had studied, speaks a real word of wisdom (*cf.* Acts 5: 34-39). He warns the Sanhedrin to be careful. He tells them that, if this enterprise of Jesus' followers is of only human origin, it will die out, but if it is from God, it will endure. And if the Sanhedrin members insist on opposing it, they could find themselves fighting against God. That's wise counsel.

Wise or not, the members of the Sanhedrin choose to fight against God anyway. They have the Apostles flogged. The latter are joyful to be able to join their sufferings to those of Jesus. They are delighted. Thrilled. That's an interesting response, isn't it? They are whipped, and happy about it!

But that is what Jesus says, isn't it? *Blessed are you when they insult you and persecute you and utter every kind of slander against you because of me. Be glad and rejoice, for your reward is great in heaven* (Matt 5:11). So they rejoice. I'm not sure I could rejoice after being whipped, but I like to think I would give it the old college try.

The Church goes on to experience more difficulty—internal squabbling (*cf.* Acts 6:1-7). At that time, virtually all of the original Christians were Jewish. But not all Jews were natives of Palestine. Many were from other lands.

As the story unfolds, a disagreement occurs between those who speak Aramaic, the language of the Jews in Palestine, and those who speak Greek, the language of the empire. The Greek-speaking Jews claim their widows aren't being treated fairly.

How typical that is. No matter how committed we are to the Lord, we can get to arguing and dividing over the darndest things. We all have our own peculiar sensitivities.

They ended by appointing seven deacons to take care of the temporal matters so that the elders of the community could give themselves more fully to their main tasks—prayer and the service of the Word (*cf.* Acts 6:1-7).

I'm convinced they were hearing very clearly from the Lord. The Church's elders (priests) are not supposed to be doing everything. But too often that's just what we try to do.

Archbishop Plourde used to urge us to call people into ministry. We should not assume, he would say, that priests have all the gifts for the apostolate. Most of the gifts for ministry, in fact, reside not in the clergy, but with the lay members of the Church.

The clergy, of course, are vital. We are the fathers of God's people on earth. We're supposed to lead. But we're not supposed to dominate. We're not supposed to do everything, even though many of the good parish folks still think we should.

The day after I arrived at St. Mary's, someone said to me: "Father, there's no holy water in the font." I thought to myself: "Wow! Am I supposed to do that?" It's not as though I mind doing stuff like that. I don't regard it as below me. But I don't think I'm supposed to do it.

The early Church started off with a prophetic stance, challenging the establishment to get back on track.

In Acts 7, the deacon Stephen addresses the Sanhedrin. He lays into them. He calls them a stiff-necked people. He cries: *You always resist the Holy Spirit. Was there ever a prophet your fathers did not persecute? ...And now you have betrayed and murdered* [*the Righteous One*] (Acts 7:51-52 NIV). They are cut to the quick and stone him to death.

The pattern is established. The stronger the stand the Church takes against the ways of the world, the tougher the harassment.

After the death of Stephen, a general persecution breaks out against the Church. All the believers, except the Apostles, scatter to the four winds. A spirit of discouragement sets in. They would need strong leadership to help them get by.

But, when persecution closes things down in one place, the Lord initiates works of power in another.

Though things look bleak, Philip, another one of the deacons, goes down to Samaria (*cf.* Acts 8:4-13). Philip exercises a powerful ministry there and many people seek Baptism.

Peter and John are sent from Jerusalem to check out what is happening in Samaria (*cf.* Acts 8:14-25). They lay hands on people there and the Holy Spirit is poured out. There is such an obvious manifestation of the power of God that one of the men of the place, Simon the magician, wants to buy the power if they can show him how to use it. Needless to say, the Apostles have some well-chosen words for him.

Philip's amazing ministry continues on a southbound road (*cf.* Acts 8:26-40). He speaks with an Ethiopian who is reading from the prophet Isaiah. Philip asks him, *"Do you understand what you are reading?" "How can I* [*understand*] *unless I have someone to guide me?"* (Acts 8:30-31 JB) the other man replies. The Ethiopian does not assume that he can simply go to the Word of God and put it all together himself. He knows he needs some teaching. The Church has always held the Scriptures in highest regard, but there is a teaching authority Jesus has established. We can read. We can study. We can be inspired by the Bible. It is, of course, God's Word. But we can't assume that we can always interpret it correctly for ourselves. We have to be taught.

From earliest days the Church has been harassed. As Acts 9 recounts, Saul the persecutor, is heading to Damascus to hunt down the Christians. Just outside Damascus, he has a vision of Jesus himself. My sense is that Saul was haunted by the face of Stephen. He had seen this young man die a violent death with an incredible peace. I presume that all the way from Jerusalem to Damascus Saul was saying to God: "Lord, can you explain to me the actions of this Stephen? What is at work? Is there any possibility, Lord, that what he was saying could be true? It can't be true! It contradicts everything I've been taught. But how was it possible for him to be the way he was?"

The Lord takes over and Saul has a powerful conversion experience. Extraordinary. He is transformed and is never the same again.

Because he has lost his sight, Saul is led into town by the hand and put under the authority of one of the elders in the Church in Damascus. Ananias prays for him and Saul regains his sight.

Once converted, Saul has only a limited ministry in Damascus and eventually has to escape from town in a basket. He heads back to Jerusalem, but his life is in danger there as well. Those who don't like the Gospel see in this convert a tremendous threat. So, for safekeeping, the Apostles send him some six hundred miles away to Tarsus, his hometown in Cilicia. They tell him to stay there until someone calls for him, and he goes. He learns very quickly what it means to be obedient.

The Church has always been characterized by effective ministry. In Joppa, Peter has a vision. In Caesarea, a Roman centurion named Cornelius likewise has a vision. The Lord puts the two of them together, and Peter finds himself preaching the Gospel to pagans. He can't believe that the Lord wants to convert non-Jews. His vision is narrow. God's vision is always wider than ours. We have to open up to the full vision of God. Peter ministers to the people and they become filled with the Holy Spirit, just the way he and the other 120 were at Pentecost.

Can we learn from this? Peter goes back to Jerusalem and has to account for what has happened. His brothers in Christ don't want to hear that the Greeks have come to the Lord. Some of them are getting too comfortable with the way things are, and are unwilling to see any change.

The Church has never been free from internal controversy. Now that all kinds of non-Jews are responding to the Gospel, the question is: Do they have to become Jewish in order to be Christians? Some say yes; others say no. How do they settle it? All the Apostles and presbyters come together in council in Jerusalem (*cf.* Acts 15).

Peter takes the floor; then Barnabas speaks. Paul, too, has his say. They talk, they pray, they listen, and then they talk some more. They have a long, long meeting. (Have we ever wished the Lord would deliver us from long meetings? I have, but I don't think he's going to. In order to pursue the work of the Kingdom, we've got to meet together whether we like it or not).

They finally make a decision, and it is proclaimed, not by Peter, nor by Paul, but by James, who is the presiding elder in Jerusalem at the time, or, as we would call him now, the Bishop. He starts by saying: *It has been decided by the Holy Spirit and by us...* (Acts 15:28 JB). The Church works with guidance of the Holy Spirit. We have to listen. We have to pray. We have to yield. And only then will the Holy Spirit will give us the Word.

Is this what has happened in Christian history? Yes, at times. But not always. We've too often settled disputes rather by splitting and going our own separate ways. Such behaviour is not reflected in the New Testament. That is not God's way, but that's what we've done. I don't know how it's going to get repaired. We ourselves can't repair it. Only God can do that.

It was the Father's plan that Jesus preach to the House of Israel only. It was given to those whom he left behind to go to the ends of the earth. Before Jesus left them, he gave them their final instructions: *Go, therefore and make disciples of all nations [and] baptize them* (Matt 28:19). *Wait in the city for the fulfillment of the Father's promise. Not many days hence you will be baptized with the Holy Spirit* (Acts 1:4-5 paraphrase). *When the Holy Spirit comes upon you, you will receive power. Then you will be my witnesses not only in Jerusalem, but throughout Judea and Samaria, and indeed to the ends of the earth* (Acts 1:8 JB). *Remain here in the city until you are clothed with power from on high* (Luke 24:49).

Nowhere do we read in the inspired Word that Jesus tells his followers to write things down. He didn't tell them not to either, but the priority is to be a body of people, to be faithful to the Lord and to move at the direction of the Holy Spirit within the structures that Jesus has left his Church.

Jesus knew the Scriptures thoroughly. He quoted continually from them, the Jewish Scriptures that is. I find it interesting that there is no record that he carried the Scriptures around with him. Not that there's anything wrong with carrying a Bible, but it wasn't necessarily the mark of someone who knew the Scriptures well. When Jesus was quoting from the Scriptures, he seldom identified where the lines came from. And again, not that there's anything wrong with identifying the reference, but it was obviously not one of Jesus' priorities.

With the coming of the Holy Spirit, the Church was launched into life and began to work in power. It was vital and it was dynamic. There were clear lines of authority. St. Paul makes that evident in his writings (*cf.* Heb 13:17). The New Testament was written out of the lived experience of the Church at the prompting of the Holy Spirit. The inspired writings were not offered in the beginning as the blueprint from which to construct the Church. The Church was not made out of the writings. The writings came out of the Church. It's important to keep that in mind. As was the case with the Old Testament, each one of the books of the New Testament was written for a specific purpose. John's Gospel, for example, was not written to provide a chronicle of Jesus' life. John says that the whole world could not contain the books that would have to be written for that (*cf.* John 21:25). It was written that we might believe (*cf.* John 20:31).

The New Testament was confided to the Church's care. It was discerned by the Church. It was preserved by the Church. It has been understood by the Church, interpreted and taught by the Church. Sacred Scripture has played a central role in the Catholic Church down through the ages. The documents of the Church are replete with references to the Scriptures. The Church teaches from the Scriptures continually.

The documents of the New Testament were not put together as we know them until late in the Fourth Century A.D. For 350 years or so after the ascension of Jesus, there were over 100 documents in various places which claimed divine inspiration. The names of some of them—the Revelation of Stephen, the Apocalypse of Paul, the Epistle to the Laodiceans, the Gospel of Bartholomew, the story of Joseph of Arimethea, the Gospel of Nicodemus, the Gospel of James, the Gospel of Thomas, the Gospel of Matthias, the Gospel of Philip. They all make interesting reading and, no doubt, have varying degrees of authenticity. But the Church did not discern them as God's own Word.

It was the teaching authority of the Church, prompted and led by the Holy Spirit, that discerned that the 27 documents that now make up the New Testament were inspired. It is the people of the Church under the inspiration of the Spirit that has written and discerned the New Testament and preserved it to the present day.

How often have disputes over various verses of the Bible split the Church? Too often. This is not God's intention. How are we supposed to settle these differences? We are supposed to come together, as Acts 15 instructs us, and pray. We are to meet with one another, listen to the Lord, and make a decision. In no way are we to divide and move off on our own. Yet, this is what we've done. This is part of the sinfulness of the Church. We are a sinful people. We have to face up to it in repentance, come humbly to the Lord and allow him to do what he wants with us.

Here are a few lines from the official prayer book of the Church—the breviary. Religious and those who are ordained, such as deacons and priests, pray from this book every day, as do a number of lay people as well. The following is from the writings of St. Ignatius, Bishop of Antioch.

He was martyred in the coliseum in Rome in 107 A.D., about 65 years or so after the death of Jesus himself. There is good reason to believe that he was evangelized and baptized by John the Apostle. So he's very connected to the early Church.

> "Hear your bishop, that God may hear you. My life is a sacrifice for those who are obedient to the bishop, the presbyters and the deacons; and may it be my lot to share with them in God. Work together in harmony, struggle together, run together, suffer together, rest together, rise together, as stewards, advisors and ser-

> vants of God. Seek to please him whose soldiers you are and from whom you draw your pay."[2]

The structures we are familiar with today are rooted soundly in the very early Church. From the beginning, the Church has been hierarchical.

From all his disciples, Jesus picked twelve. From the twelve, he chose three—Peter, James and John—for specific things. And out of these three he picked Peter for a particular role. Three times he asked Peter, *Do you love me?* and then said, *Feed my sheep* (*cf.* John 21:15-17). The Good Shepherd left another shepherd in his place, and a whole line of shepherds down through the ages. History tells us that Peter was succeeded as Bishop in Rome by Linus, then by Cletus, and then by Clement, whose writings are still with us. Earlier, Paul had reprimanded the Church in Corinth. In 95 A.D., or so, Clement had to reprimand them again. He took them to task for various things even though it is entirely likely the Apostle John was still alive. Clement was able to speak with authority from Rome to the Church in Corinth because he was the successor of Peter.

Unity and obedience have always been big in the Church. Jesus himself said: *The scribes and the Pharisees occupy the chair of Moses. You must therefore do what they tell you and listen to what they say* (Matt 23:2-3 JB). That's an awfully strong word on obedience, considering the other things he had said about the scribes and the Pharisees. Lawful authority within the Church was not to depend on the worthiness of the authorities themselves.

When Peter and the others received the Holy Spirit at Pentecost, the chair of Moses passed from the Jewish authorities to them. That's why Peter was able to say to the Sanhedrin: *Is it right for*

2 St. Ignatius of Antioch, *Letter to Polycarp*, 5, 1-8, 1. 3, as quoted in *The Liturgy of the Hours*, Vol. III, p. 568.

us to obey you rather than God (Acts 4:19 paraphrase)? Authority had been taken away from the Sanhedrin and given to him and the Apostles.

Vatican II was all about renewal. We can easily get into a rut in the Church if we slip away from God's purposes and become comfortable. We can assume that he's opted out and is not speaking or doing anything anymore. At the inauguration of the Council, Pope John XXIII said that "we must open the windows and let the Holy Spirit blow through." Then the Pope led delegates in this prayer: "Renew your wonders, O Lord, in our day as in a new Pentecost."

I believe that today we are on the brink of the new Pentecost in the Church. We have seen a lot of good things happen when people try to be as faithful as they can to the Lord. Yet I believe we haven't seen anything compared to what we are going to see as time goes on. We are going to see a time when the Gospel will be lived and spoken with power. Even at my advanced age, I believe I will live to see it.

We need renewal and revival today because our present agenda is not working very well. Are we satisfied with the condition of the Church? Are we satisfied with the condition of our parishes? Are we satisfied with the condition of our families? Are we satisfied with the condition of our own lives? Is God satisfied? Not a chance. Do we think he has the power to change things? Of course he has. The key question is: are we willing to let God exercise his power?

We are meant to be a beacon to those around us. We fall short of that. But, as we submit to the Lord, he purifies us and brings us together. People will be attracted by the light of the Gospel as they see it in our lives. They will come and become one with us.

Study Questions:

1 Fr. Bob is obviously in love with the Church: "The fact that the Church is sinful and human is no reason for abandoning it... It's easier to be critical than to get involved... The Church would be an incredible place if it weren't for the people. That's human nature. We have to love the Church... God calls for us to love the Church with all its spots, wrinkles and barnacles. Do we love the Church?"

Ask the Lord for the gift to love his Church.

2 Fr. Bob says, "Our 'ineffectiveness quotient' is in direct proportion to our resistance to his Word. We are rebellious people. We like to do things our own way... But don't we realize this is the root of sin? God has a plan, but our willfulness gets in his way... How powerful God would be able to work through us if only we could be fully submitted to his Word."

In order to 'be Church', we need to let go of some of our preferences and adopt an attitude of cheerful willingness and obedience to God's Word.

Where are the "spots, wrinkles and barnacles" in you where God is asking you to choose obedience?

3 Fr. Bob says, "We need renewal and revival today because our present agenda is not working very well. Are we satisfied with the condition of the Church? Are we satisfied with the condition of our parishes? Are we satisfied with the condition of our families? Are we satisfied with the condition of our own lives? Is God satisfied? Not a chance... The key question is: are we willing to let God exercise his power?"

What does it mean for you to let God exercise his power?

CHAPTER FIVE

Liturgy

Ritual is very human. The Jewish people had plenty of ritual, and the Christian Church has developed it over the centuries under the guidance of the Holy Spirit.

We're not alone, however. There is a lot of non-religious ritual in our society as well. We actually should be used to it. We have parades and presentations and royalty. We have daily proceedings of Parliament. The inauguration of the President in the United States is ritual. The Order of Canada, the mayor's robes and chain of office, the Changing of the Guard—all ritual. Ritual is natural and normal. It should not, then, be surprising if we ritualize our worship of God.

But dead ritual is bad. That's the kind of ritual that is mere ceremony. It doesn't really mean anything. We perform bad ritual by rote, out of obligation, to justify ourselves because we're supposed to, out of custom, or out of fear. Some churches have abolished ritual because they've concluded from their unsatisfying experiences of it that it's of no use. But that's like throwing the baby out with the bath.

Catholic churches still have a fair bit of ritual. We believe that it has good roots in the history of God's people. From the very beginning, the believers in Jesus have gathered together to celebrate the mysteries of God in what has come to be called the Liturgy of the Church.

A mystery, by the way, is not something one can't understand, but a truth that is so profound that it requires revelation.

The Eucharist

In Acts 2:42, Luke lists four things that the original believers did together. One of them is *the breaking of the bread*, which we understand as the Eucharist. The Eucharist has been the principal celebration of God's people over the centuries. A document which dates back to the very early part of the second century called *The Teaching of the Twelve Apostles* or *The Didache*, provides detailed instructions as to how the Eucharist is to be celebrated. The third and fourth generations of Christians celebrated it basically the same way that we celebrate it today. They came together, sang an entrance song and went into repentance mode. The president of the assembly—the "principal celebrant" as we call him now—took over then and called them to praise. He then introduced a prayer which led into the reading of the Word of God. After the presider had commented on them, preparation of the altar began. The gifts of bread and wine were brought forward and the prayer of thanksgiving was said over them (words of institution). Communion was then celebrated and the assembly was adjourned.

The Eucharist is called a sacrifice and so it is. Yet there is only one sacrifice of the New Law, the sacrifice of Jesus Christ himself. The shedding of his blood at Calvary was sufficient to accomplish the salvation of the whole world. What we do at the Eucharist is to make that sacrifice present again and again. We are not multiplying sacrifices, as many people, who don't understand what we're doing, tell us. We are re-presenting the one sacrifice of Christ. Why? Because Jesus has told us to. The name 'Eucharist' comes from a Greek word meaning 'giving thanks'. We give thanks to God for the salvation that Jesus has won upon the Cross, and we make present again the one sufficient sacrifice of Jesus. We are simply being obedient to his command.

St. Paul says that Jesus is *a priest forever according to the order of Melchizedek* (Heb 6:20), as did the psalmist in prophesying about the Messiah hundreds of years before he came (Ps 110:4). If we want to find out about Melchizedek, we have to go back to the Book of Genesis. This very mysterious chap appeared out of nowhere to meet with Abraham, who had been sent by God from Ur of the Chaldeans to what the Lord called the "Promised Land"—the land flowing with milk and honey where the Lord himself would found a race of people whose descendants would be as numerous as the sands of the seashore. This was a very unlikely prospect considering that Abraham was over seventy at the time, and didn't have any children. And yet it happened.

Abraham left home *not knowing where he was going* (Heb 11:8). I love that description because I can relate to it. So often I don't know where I am going. I may be quite sure that the Lord is directing me because I've prayed. I'm peaceful about it, and those whom I'm close to agree with me—good signs that the Lord is in charge. But very often I don't know where I'm going to get to.

As Abraham journeyed along, the Lord sent him the unusual and mysterious Melchizedek, who offered him bread and wine. Abraham, in turn, gave him a tithe, which is something Jews were taught to offer to the Levites, the priests of the temple. So whoever he was, he was a priest of some kind. On the night before he died, Jesus called his twelve around him in the paschal meal setting, and he confected what we call the Sacrament of the Eucharist: *This is my body, this is my blood* (*cf.* Matt 26:26-28). Jesus established the Eucharist by changing the bread and wine into his own body and blood, the *bread of life* (John 6:35).

From the rising of the sun, to the going down thereof... a clean offering is given in sacrifice to my name (Mal 1:11 paraphrase). Bread and wine would certainly qualify. What has happened in the Christian Church ever since the beginning is the offering of the clean sacrifice of bread and wine, simply a re-presenting of the one sacrifice of Jesus upon the Cross. And we do this at his command. *Do this in memory of me* (Luke 22:19 NABRE).

Every time you eat this bread and drink this cup, you proclaim the death of the Lord, until he comes [again] (1 Cor 11:26). We believe that Jesus is truly present in the bread and the wine. We believe that this is not just a symbol, but something very real. In fact, there is nothing else like it. The word 'Sacrament', meaning sacred moment or encounter, was coined to describe special celebrations in the experience of Christian people. The Eucharist is a sacramental presence. It's not physical as we are present to one another or as Jesus was when he walked upon earth. But, nonetheless, Jesus is fully present in the elements.

The Eucharist is something only God could have thought of. It is the kind of gift we would give to someone after we had already given him/her everything we could think of. St. Paul expresses it most clearly. *Is not the cup of blessing we bless a sharing in the blood of Christ? And is not the bread we break a sharing in the body of Christ* (1 Cor 10:16)?

Today we speak of seven special celebrations that we call Sacraments, the Eucharist being one. These developed over the course of the Church's history as she tried to be faithful to what the Lord had commissioned her to do.

There is power in the Eucharist that we celebrate together. And that power is released by God as people of faith gather in obedience to his command with a spirit of expectation. If we don't experience the power of the Lord through the celebration of the Eucharist, I truly believe that one of the main reasons is that we don't expect it. Do we expect something to happen when we come to celebrate the mysteries of God? We should. When that starts to take hold in an assembly, then the Lord begins to move. Faith is so important. He wants us to believe.

When people come together in faith and expectation, then the power of God is released. We've seen that in the Eucharistic celebrations at St. Mary's. We have had people converted to the Lord just by being here in celebration with us. We've seen healings happen. The Eucharist is supposed to be a very revealing experience. We don't come together principally to experience the power of God. We come together to worship him in obedience. But as we do that, I believe we're supposed to see the power of God in our assemblies. When the early Christians gathered together, the walls shook. That was a lively Church! That's the way it's supposed to be. I haven't seen the walls shake at St. Mary's yet, but if they do some day, I'll say: "There's precedent for that. It's happened before."

Baptism

Baptism is a ritual of initiation. There are clear references in Scripture to Baptism. The symbolism is powerful, linking the dying and the rising of Christ with the individual believer. *Are you not aware that we who were baptized into Christ Jesus were baptized into his death* (Rom 6:3)? We celebrate the victory that Jesus has won through his death. At Baptism, we are come forth from the water in the fullness of his life.

Baptism is also a receiving of the Holy Spirit. At Pentecost, when Peter gave his very first exhortation, some of those in the crowd were convicted. They said, What must we do? His answer was, *Repent, and be baptized every one of you in the name of Jesus Christ for the forgiveness of your sins; and you shall receive the gift of the Holy Spirit* (Acts 2:38 RSV). And Jesus told them: *Go and make disciples of all the nations. Baptize them in the name of the Father, and of the Son, and of the Holy Spirit* (Matt 28:19).

As Catholics, we baptize infants. There are some who take issue with this practice. I remember talking to a couple who belonged to another church. They said: "We respect what you do, but we don't do it ourselves. We believe that when you baptize a baby, all you have is a wet baby." But we think we see indications in Scripture about the baptizing of children and infants in the references to the baptizing of whole households. St. Paul didn't do much baptizing, but in 1 Cor 1:16 he said: *I baptized the household of Stephanas,* and in Acts 16:15, he baptized Lydia, the purple-cloth merchant from Thyatira, and her household. In Acts 16:33, the jailer and his whole household were baptized. Were there no children there? As in most ordinary households, we assume there were children.

The ideal is clear. When we baptize an infant, it is baptized into the death of Jesus and surrendered to the care of a family of faith. The family prays for him or her along with the Church, and nurtures the gift as the years go on. Because the child grows up knowing the Lord right from his or her earliest days, there isn't any real need for a spiritual awakening somewhere down the line. Everything happens naturally. When the gifts of the Holy Spirit are supposed to be activated, they'll be activated. In actuality, we are a long way from the ideal. Not all children are brought up in families of fervent faith. But that's the way it's supposed to be. The baptism of infants makes sense.

Confirmation

Confirmation, another of our celebrations includes the laying on of hands, anointing with oil, and praying for the outpouring of the Holy Spirit. The Holy Spirit is confided to me in the Sacrament of Baptism like a Christmas present all wrapped up and with a bow tied 'round it, and a card with my name on it. It's mine, but until I unwrap it and begin to use it, I don't really have it fully. The Holy Spirit that I receive at Baptism needs the Sacrament of Confirmation as a stirring up in order to change me and get me ready to minister in the name of the Lord.

Confirmation is one of the Sacraments of Initiation. *As Paul laid his hands on them, the Holy Spirit [descended upon] them, and they began to speak in tongues and to utter prophecies* (Acts 19:6). Paul laid his hands on them, and the Holy Spirit came. In the early Church, infants were confirmed, as they still are today in the Eastern Church where infants are 'chrismated', that is, anointed with oil. Infants are given the Eucharist as well. The Eastern Church regards both of these rituals as Sacraments of Initiation. *He who anoints us has sealed us with the first payment—the Spirit in our hearts* (2 Cor 1:22). Paul also teaches, *When you heard the glad tidings of salvation, the word of truth, and believed in it, you were sealed with the Holy Spirit who had been promised* (Eph 1:13). *Do nothing to sadden the Holy Spirit with whom you were sealed* (Eph 4:30). Confirmation seals and protects me, and gives me a guard which I can call upon.

Reconciliation

The Sacrament of Reconciliation has an interesting history. Perhaps we read stories of public penance where people used to write their sins on cards which they carried with them in full view so that everybody knew. Confessing sins to one another is also mentioned in James 5:16.

The Sacrament of Reconciliation can be a great healing encounter if it is approached in faith. I have seen people touched and healed of the roots of some of their sins in celebrating the Sacrament of Reconciliation with expectant faith. I've had people come back and talk to me about the first anniversary of their victory over something they were struggling with:

> "Father, this is my anniversary."
> "Anniversary? What are you talking about? You're not even married."
> "A year ago today we celebrated the Sacrament of Reconciliation together. Do you remember what I talked about and what I was burdened with."

"Oh, yes. I do remember now."
"Victory. A whole year! Total victory."

I've gone through similar conversations again and again. That is what the Sacrament of Reconciliation is for. It has come out of lived experience of the Church under the guidance of the Holy Spirit.

Anointing of the Sick

James 5:14 refers to the Anointing of the Sick: *Is there anyone sick among you? He should ask for the presbyters of the Church. They in turn are to pray over him, anointing him with oil in the name of the Lord.*

Matrimony and Holy Orders

The other two Sacraments of Matrimony and Holy Orders grew out of the history of the Church to identify, in a special way, anointed moments in our Christian lives. *While they were engaged in the liturgy of the Lord and were fasting, the Holy Spirit spoke to them: "Set apart Barnabas and Saul for me to do the work for which I have called them"* (Acts 13:2).

The Sabbath

A local church frequently advertises in the paper: "When Jesus was on earth he went to church on Saturday. Won't you come and join us on Saturday as we worship the Lord?" It is true that when Jesus was on earth, he did go to church (synagogue) on Saturday. However, the early Church celebrated the Breaking of the Bread on the first day of the week (Acts 20:7) for several reasons. First, it was the day on which the Lord rose from the dead. While the Sabbath was the last day of the week of the first creation, the Lord's Day is the first day of the new creation inaugurated by Christ's resurrection. In Christ, the spiritual meaning of the Sabbath is fully realized. In addition, the earliest Christians, as faithful Jews, wanted to worship on the last day of the week in their synagogues.

Sacramentals

As Catholics, we are familiar with sacred things which we sometimes call 'sacramentals', the principal ones being water, oil, and salt. Water symbolizes life; oil symbolizes strength; salt symbolizes protection. We are also familiar with relics, such as the handkerchiefs that were touched to Paul's person. *When handkerchiefs or cloths which had touched his [Paul's] skin were applied to the sick, their diseases were cured and evil spirits departed from them* (Acts 19:12). The Lord is able to invest material things with his power. The Church uses these things in faith. We are not disembodied spirits. We are people made of flesh and blood who live in this world and have to deal with it. This is where the whole business of artifacts and pictures comes in. We don't pray to pictures or statues. We don't worship things like that. They have their place and can be useful as reminders. These things have been learned by the Church as we have journeyed forward with the Lord.

Purgatory

We are all under the sentence of death, are we not? Death is not God's idea. Death has come into the world because we have rebelled against God—the original sin. We should not start blaming our first parents, because we have all participated in the original sin. We have all rebelled against God in one way or other. *All have sinned and fall short of the glory of God* (Rom 3:23 RSV). So we are all under the same sentence. The world looks upon death as being the end, especially when it happens to younger people. The death of a young person is always tragic and can be difficult for those who remain, because we finish with an empty place in our lives and in our hearts. The Lord has built into us a grieving process that is good, healthy, and important. We become nervous when somebody suffers a loss of a loved one and doesn't grieve. We can't suppress grief without paying a price. That's the way the Lord has built us.

As believers, we have a view of death that is different from the world's. Death is not difficult for those who die in the Lord. For those who die in him, it's something to look forward to—a joyful passage. Are we looking forward to that passage? I don't think most of us are. I think we are still very tied to what we are doing here. Things aren't over when we go through that passage; in fact, things are just beginning. Catherine Doherty, the founder of the Madonna House community in Combermere, said as she was approaching the end of her life:

> "Don't try to hold me here. Don't pray for me to get better and get healed. I'm 87 years old and I'm ready to go."
> "But we'll miss you."
> "That's all right. You'll manage, and I'll be able to do much better work in heaven."

That is the way we need to look at death.

Jesus said, *Be perfect as your heavenly Father is perfect* (Matt 5:48 JB). In order to live in God's house, we have to be perfect; otherwise we won't fit in. We can be made perfect through the merits of Jesus Christ, but in spite of our prayer, in spite of our ministry, in spite of our pilgrimages, in spite of everything, we know we are not perfect yet. *There is a war going on within me. I don't always do the thing I want to do, I wind up doing the evil I do not intend* (Rom 7:19 Fr. Bob trans). The great St. Paul struggled, and we can infer what his temptations might have been if we read his letters. He was impatient and impulsive. We have only to read some of the things he says in Galatians 5.

In order to live with the Lord, we have to be perfect. What happens when we die? Are we immediately perfected, just like that? I suppose that's possible, but the Church has come to understand that normally a process of purification is necessary. This is a gift from God to get us ready to live with him forever. The process is called purgatory, and it deals with those problems in our lives that we didn't have time to deal with when we were here on earth. It is not well understood by those who don't believe. We will hear people criticize the Catholic Church for teaching a doctrine of second chance. Purgatory has nothing to do with a second chance. There is only one chance, and that is here on earth. The Church has never taught anything different. Some people think it's the Lord beating up on us in order to get even for the things that we've done wrong. How dare they teach a cruel God like that! Purgatory is a loving, purifying experience. The suffering involved is the intense longing to be with the Lord.

Sometimes purifying experiences can be painful. If we've ever been sick, we've probably surrendered ourselves to the medics. We trust that they will make us better, but accept the reality that sometimes the process can be painful. I can still remember the castor oil I used to have to take when I was a youngster. It was given in love and I knew somehow it was good for me, but still I didn't like it. In fact, it was quite nasty.

There are a couple of passages in the Bible that may be references to what we talk of as purgatory. They are in the Deuterocanonical (Protestants call them apocryphal) books of the Bible. I suppose this is as good a time as any to discuss the two canons of Scripture. Have we ever heard the expressions "Catholic Bible" and "Protestant Bible" as though there were two different Bibles? There is only one Word of God. The Catholic version includes what are known as the Deuterocanonicals (Tobit, Judith, 1 and 2 Maccabees, Baruch, Wisdom, Sirach, and portions of Esther and Daniel), which don't occur in Protestant versions. Why? It goes back to the very beginning of the Church.

In the time of Jesus, various groups of Jews (e.g. Sadducees, Pharisees, Essenes, Diaspora Jews) had different ideas about which writings were considered Scripture. There was no Jewish canon (list of authoritative books) at that time. All Jews considered the first five books (the Torah or Pentateuch) to be central to their faith. After these, the Prophets came next in importance.

The status of other writings was in dispute. It was not until the 2nd century A.D. that the Jews decided on a collection of books as canonical, which did not include the Deuterocanonicals.

However, the canon chosen by the Jewish authorities was not binding on Christians, since Jesus gave that authority to the Apostles and their successors (cf. Matt 21:33-45). Among Christians in the West, there were disputes over which books to include in both the Old and New Testament canons up to the 4th century A.D.

During this time the Deuterocanonicals were read in public worship throughout the early Church which is evidence that she recognized them as the inspired Word of God. Regional Councils at Rome (382), Hippo (393) and Carthage (397, 419) endorsed the practice of the Church at the time, listing all the Deuterocanonicals in the canon, concluding, "we have received from our fathers that those books must be read in the Church."[3] Because of their widespread influence, these declarations ended the canonical disputes in the West.

In July 1519, Johann Maier von Eck confronted Martin Luther with the text of 2 Maccabees 12:43-45 in a debate in Leipzig on the nature of purgatory. Luther responded that 2 Maccabees was not in the canon of Scripture. Eventually, he and other Reformers declared the Deuterocanonicals to be apocryphal (not canonical). In light of this controversy, the Council of Trent reaffirmed the traditional list of canonical books in an authoritative statement in 1546, pointing to the Church's long-established usage of these books.

There is a rather clear intimation of Purgatory in 2 Maccabees, where Judas Maccabeus takes up a collection to provide for an expiatory sacrifice on behalf of soldiers who had died:

3 *Council of Carthage*, canon 47.

> *He then took up a collection among all his soldiers, amounting to two thousand silver drachmas, which he sent to Jerusalem to provide for an expiatory sacrifice. In doing this, he acted in a very excellent and noble way, inasmuch as he had the resurrection of the dead in view. For if he were not expecting the fallen to rise again, it would have been useless and foolish to pray for them in death. But if he did this with a view to the splendid reward that awaits those who have gone to rest in godliness, it was a holy and pious thought. Thus, he made atonement for the dead, that they might be freed from* this *sin* (2 Mac 12:42-46).

The Apostle Paul says something very peculiar, *If the dead are not raised, what about those who have themselves baptized on behalf of the dead* (1 Cor 15:29)? The practice of people being baptized in proxy for those who had died was common in the early Church in some places. It did not endure too long. The early Church ruled it out of order. But Paul doesn't really comment on it. Instead, he uses it as a basis of a teaching on the resurrection of Christ.

Heaven

Those who refuse the Lord's offer of life have condemned themselves to experience the permanent absence of the Lord. That's hell. Those who accept the salvation that Jesus has won and live it out in God's grace will have every tear wiped away and will experience total fulfilment in heaven.

However, once we get to heaven, we won't be just resting. Some of my students used to say: "I'm not very interested in heaven, because I'm not sure if I want to sit around playing a harp all day." There is a reference to playing harps in the Scriptures (Rev 15:2), but it's only a symbol for praising God. The basic activity of heaven will be the praise of God. If we have ever lost ourselves in praising him, and sensed our whole beings lifted up, then the Lord has given us a small taste of heaven. There is ultimately no more satisfying human experience than praising God.

When we praise God, we are at our finest. Praise of God expresses best the relationship between God and man. There is no better expression of my relationship to God than when I am singing to his glory. We do it at Mass. We sing: "Glory to God in the highest, and peace to his people on earth. We worship you. We give you thanks. We praise you..."

Communion of Saints

But that's not all that's going on in heaven. John, the visionary, sees four living creatures and twenty-four elders before the throne of God (Rev 5:8). The four living creatures—a lion, a calf, an eagle, and a human being—can be considered symbols, or characteristics of the people of God—strength, obedience, swiftness, and a likeness unto him. The twenty-four represent twelve patriarchs and twelve Apostles. Twenty-four is a biblical (or symbolic) number occurring only in the Book of Revelation. These animals and elders are portrayed as giving praise and glory before the throne of God in two specific ways—playing harps and offering bowls of incense.

Playing the harp is a symbol for praising God and the smoke of incense is a biblical image for people's prayers ascending to God. Although the symbolism is clear, John goes on to explain: *This incense* [*represents*] *the prayers of the saints* (Rev 5:8 JB). The word 'saint' was used in the New Testament to describe a believer on earth, not in heaven. So the two things that the people in heaven are doing are praising God and offering to him the prayers of those on earth. This speaks rather clearly to what we call the communion of saints—the communion of the saints on earth with the saints in heaven. The communion of the saints has been a teaching of the Church from earliest times.

The author of the letter to the Hebrews has something very

interesting to say. Here is a slightly expanded and paraphrased version. You have drawn near to Mount Zion (this is one of the phrases for God's place), the city of the living God, the heavenly Jerusalem, and close to myriads (millions upon millions) of angels in festal gathering. You have been drawn close to the spirits of just men who have gone on before you, finished their purification, and in their perfection now reside in the presence of God, the judge of all. You are in communion with them, and with Jesus, the mediator of a new covenant, and with the sprinkled blood which speaks more eloquently than that of Abel (*cf.* Heb 12:22-24). This passage is highly descriptive and poetic, but is significant, I believe, in that it seems to speak directly to the communion of saints.

Mary

Finally, we need to have a look at the place of Mary, the mother of Jesus.

We believe that in the communion of all believers, she stands ahead of everyone else. In humility, she has said that she is nothing: *For he has regarded the low estate of his handmaiden. For behold, henceforth all generations will call me blessed; For he who is mighty has done great things for me* (Luke 1:48-49 RSV). Do we want to be part of a generation which doesn't call her blessed? If we are going to be faithful to the Lord, we have to call her blessed. It isn't just a matter of saying, "Yes, Mary is blessed." We have to call it out: "Blessed!" just as the Angel Gabriel did. *Blessed are you among women* (Luke 1:28). And Elizabeth, her cousin too: *And blessed is she who believed that there would be a fulfillment of what was spoken to her from the Lord* (Luke 1:45 RSV). Mary believed the Word of God, and she was blessed because of it.

The Catholic Church teaches that Mary was preserved free from sin from the first moment of her existence. In the first book of the Bible, the Lord addresses Satan in words like the following:

You have won a victory, but it is not the final triumph. I will win that. I will place enmity between you and the woman, between your seed and hers (*cf.* Gen 3:15). There will be no connection between the two. The seed who crushes the enemy's head with his heel is Jesus, the Saviour. The woman, the Saviour's mother, is Mary. The fact that there is enmity between Satan and her means he has no part of her. He cannot touch her because she is preserved by the grace of God. She is to carry within her the very Son of God. It was fitting for Jesus to be affirmed and nurtured perfectly, with no taint of the enemy's control, right from the instant of his own conception. Mary, conceived without sin, was able to do that.

But, not only do we believe that Mary was immaculately conceived. We believe also that she was graced with a complete triumph over sin and its consequences and was preserved free from the corruption of the tomb: "The Immaculate Mother of God, the ever Virgin Mary, having completed the course of her earthly life, was assumed body and soul into heavenly glory."[4]

When Jesus went up to the Mountain of Transfiguration with his Apostles, *Moses and Elijah appeared in glory...* (Luke 9:30). Moses and Elijah already in glory, even before Jesus? Very interesting! Because they are in glory they can appear to us. We believe that Mary—like Moses and Elijah—is in glory and therefore can appear to people. There are all kinds of reports of Marian apparitions around the world. It's exhausting trying to keep up with them all. I've tried. I've come to the conclusion that, although many of the reports are false, some of them are probably quite authentic.

When he departed, Jesus didn't leave his followers a detailed list of instructions and tie up everything in a neat bundle. There were many issues he did not teach about specifically. He didn't intend to. The Church would take over. Under the guidance of

4 Pope Pius XII, *Munificentissimus Deus*, 44.

the Holy Spirit, she would settle questions as they would arise through gatherings of the elders in councils (*cf.* Acts 15). It's the same today. New questions keep coming up because of the development of mankind, and we have continually to deal with them. The elders of the Church come together, they pray, they seek the Lord, they settle it, and then they teach it. That is the origin of the documents of the Church. The official teachings of the Magisterium of the Church go back to the time of the Apostles.

From the time that Jesus ascended into heaven, the Church has lived and celebrated the liturgy and evolved under the guidance of the Holy Spirit. The Eucharist has always been central to the worship of the Christian people, and the basic format—praising God, listening to his Word, the offering, the Eucharistic prayer, the communion, the dismissal—has never changed. It is important that we continue to celebrate it here on earth in anticipation of what we will one day be celebrating in heaven.

Study Questions:

1 Fr. Bob quoted Acts 2:42, which lists four essential elements of the life of the early Church: the teaching of the Apostles, the shared life, the breaking of the bread and the common prayers.

   a) How are these essential elements present in the Church today?

   b) Though the essentials remain constant, how have you experienced a diversity of expressions of these elements?

2 How does the existence of purgatory reveal the mercy of God?

3 How can expectant faith change our experience of the Sacraments?

CHAPTER SIX

Prayer

Once we see Jesus for who he really is, there is only one response that makes sense—total. Anything else is insane. Once we have set out on the road to full discipleship and opted to live it out every day, we are at the starting point. It is not the end of the line. It is just the beginning.

If the gift of the Holy Spirit is being stirred up within us, changing us, making us into a people of lively faith, enthused for the Kingdom of God, giving us a desire to share what the Lord has done, giving us a desire to serve and be used by God for his purposes—the natural response is to seek deeper and deeper communion with God. That takes us to prayer. Prayer is communion with God. That's what Pope John Paul II calls it.

The catechism I grew up with defined prayer as the raising of the mind and the heart to God. In any case, it is a two-way business. We talk and we listen.

One of the main problems most of us have in prayer is that we do lots of talking, but not much listening. But the Lord has given us a clue about it himself. We each have one mouth and two ears. We should be doing a good deal more listening than we're accustomed to.

The Lord has a tremendous desire to share his life. He longs for intimacy and friendship with each of us. Jesus said it clearly: *I no longer call you servants, but I call you friends* (John 15:15 paraphrase). Friendship with God? Amazing!

We have to follow Jesus' example. When he came to earth he was, in ways we don't really understand, separated from his Father. But he sought continual communion with him. *Jesus went out to the mountain to pray.* On this particular occasion, *he spent the* [*entire*] *night in communion with God,* [*his Father*] (Luke 6:12). *Rising early the next morning, he went off to a lonely place in the desert. There he was absorbed in prayer* (Mark 1:35).

It's interesting to note the time of day that Jesus committed to prayer—early. Was he a morning person? Not at all. He was a prayer person.

But what do I do if I'm a night person? There's a simple answer, I believe—become a morning person.

How can I do that? First of all I have to realize that getting up in the morning is not a gift. It's a decision. It's a decision that has to be made every day. When I do it often enough, I get good at it. It becomes a skill.

I speak from my own experience. When I was younger, and had the chance, I would sleep till noon. Noon! I would have to be blasted out of my comfort. I was in no way then a morning person, but that has changed. I get up early in the morning now and commit an extended time to prayer. I have become a morning person. It did not come as a gift. It came as the result of a regular decision to rise early (God's grace making it possible, of course). The Lord enabled me to develop it as a skill.

Jesus says that there has to be a quiet place for us to pray.

Whenever you pray, go to your room, close the door and pray to your Father in private (Matt 6:6). We are talking here about a time during the day when we can be quiet with the Lord, or if we want to make some noise, that we are in a position where we do not disturb too many people. Living in a family with children running around could be a problem, a problem that the Lord will help us to solve provided we make the decision that we want to do it. Whether we have to put cotton batting in our ears, or even soundproof a room, it is worth the trouble and worth the investment.

Prayer should be regarded as an appointment with God. It has to be part of my daily schedule, something that I would simply not do without. I would not think ordinarily of going without sleep over the course of a 24 hour period. I will commit time to that because I need it. Unless I am fasting for some particular reason, I would not think of going without eating, because I need it. Neither should I think of going without praying. I need it and it is that kind of conviction we have to have about it.

Even if it is dull and boring, we go to school because we want to pass and go on to the next level. If we want to make a living, we go to work. And if we want to get promoted, we get there on time and put in a decent day. School and work are necessities. So is prayer.

Jesus has something to say about the manner of praying too. *In praying do not heap up empty phrases* (Matt 6:7 RSV). Jesus is not against words. Obviously words are expressions of our thoughts. But simply repeating a series of words does not necessarily add up to a time of prayer. We can have all the devotions we like—litanies, novenas, and so on—but these things are merely a help to prayer. In themselves they are not prayer.

We must imitate Jesus' mother. *She treasured all these things and pondered them in her heart* (Luke 2:19 JB). That's prayer. That's meditation. That's coming before the Lord in peace and quiet and opening up our hearts. We can do no better than imitate Mary.

Jesus talked a lot about forgiveness. In fact, he said there wasn't much point even in trying to pray if there are some unreconciled matters extant. *When you [come] to pray, forgive anyone against whom you have a grievance* (Mark 11:25). If I do not forgive, it becomes a block between me and God.

The problem with unforgiveness is that, if I don't forgive, it will hurt me.

A young priest who ministered in Brazil for a few years recounted to me a most unusual story. He used to have a healing service every First Friday, a day given over to honouring the Sacred Heart of Jesus. He would pray for healing after Mass. People would line up across the front of the church, and the priest would go along and pray for whatever needs the people had.

One day, as he was praying for different people, he came to a young boy about 14 years of age who was on crutches. The priest could see the boy had a badly disfigured foot. An accident had caused it to turn in when he was quite young. He prayed for the obvious—that the Lord would heal the foot—and then went to move on. He was in the habit of praying as he proceeded. "Lord lead me," he would say. "Show me what to do. Show me what to pray for. Show me what the problems are."

Just as he was leaving the boy to go to the next person, he had a sense that he should stop and go back. This would happen occasionally with him, and will with any of us if we are trying to listen to the Lord. So he went back to the young man whom he did not know, and said, "Lord, what is it?" The word "Forgive" came into his mind. Accordingly, he said to the boy, "Don't you need to forgive somebody?" The boy shook his head quickly and rather angrily. "No," he said. "Nobody."

He started to leave again. But once again there was something restraining him. "Lord, what is it?" he asked. The word "father" came into his mind. So he said to the youngster, "Son, don't you need to forgive your father?" With that, the boy started to cry. The priest knew then he was on track. He said, "You need to forgive your father, don't you?" It turned out that the young man had been very badly used by his father, tragically neglected. The priest said: "Just look into my eyes, and imagine that I am your father. Say 'Daddy, I forgive you.' Can you do that?" The boy choked out the words. The foot straightened out in a matter of seconds. He left the crutches at the altar and walked out of the church.

Unforgiveness can be a block to what God wants to do in my life. If there is somebody in my life whom I have not forgiven, then I have to forgive him/her. *If you come before the altar and remember someone has a grievance against you, leave your gift at the altar and go be reconciled with your friend. Then come to the altar with your gift* (Matt 5:23-24 paraphrase). It doesn't matter how I feel. Forgiveness is not a feeling. When Jesus was hanging on the Cross, I don't think he felt like forgiving the people who were insulting him. He was dying out of love for them, and they were calling him names. I don't think he <u>felt</u> like forgiving them. But he did it anyway. *Father forgive them, for they know not what they do* (Luke 23:34 Douay). He made the decision to forgive. Forgiveness is not a feeling. Forgiveness is a decision.

To a large extent prayer is a gift, but it is also a skill that we have to develop. The disciples asked Jesus about it: *Lord,* they said to him, *teach us to pray, [just] as John taught his disciples* (Luke 11:1). At that point Jesus gave them the formula that we know and call the Lord's Prayer.

In order to begin to pray seriously, we have to be convinced of prayer's importance and make a decision about it. If we are going to be disciples of the Lord, we have to commit ourselves to some extended time in prayer. Just "Hello" and "Goodbye" to the Lord is not enough. We have to do more than that. We have to take the time to sit down, kneel down, or whatever (from personal experience I would suggest that lying down is not a good idea) and come before the Lord for some quality time.

When I was in my fourth year at the seminary, the spiritual director was a very pious, very prayerful man. He coaxed us—really put on the press—into joining what was called at that time the Priests' Eucharistic League. One of the things that we promised to do as members was to make a holy hour before the Blessed Sacrament once a week. We used to do that in the seminary on Thursdays from five to six o'clock. We promised to continue doing it after we were ordained.

About three weeks into the priesthood, after blessing just about everybody in Ottawa, I remembered my promise. "What about the holy hour? I thought. "I'd better try it." Thus, one afternoon before supper, I went over to the church to pray from five to six. I barely made it through the hour. It was torture! I could not get my head into it. I couldn't concentrate. I couldn't keep my mind on it. It was incredible! It was an exercise in endurance. It was so hard on me that I never did it again in spite of my promise. I would say to the Lord: "You know I'm busy. I'm working for you. My work is my prayer."

I didn't realize at the time what a mistake I was making. Work is not prayer. Even though it be fully dedicated to the Lord, work is not prayer. Work is work. Only prayer is prayer.

Things went downhill from there. Fifteen or so years later, I was not praying much at all. I had given up the Rosary. I had given up parts of the breviary, the Liturgy of the Hours. I was busy—working for the Lord. I knew that there was something wrong about that, something missing in my life. I knew I was supposed to pray. I thought about it. I wondered about it. I made half-hearted resolutions about it. But it didn't happen. I was not praying. I just didn't know how to do it.

In the spring of 1975, I took part in a Holy Spirit seminar. When we came to the point when we were to ask to be baptized with the Holy Spirit, we were encouraged to ask for different ministry gifts, the ones St. Paul lists in 1 Corinthians 12. I had been reading and wondering about them—healing, prophecy, tongues, and the others. I remember saying to the Lord: "If you don't want to give me any of those gifts, Lord, that's okay. But there is one thing I do need—desperately. I need a gift of prayer. I need it, and I beg for it." I didn't even know if there was such a gift.

It was amazing! Within a day, I had a hunger in my heart for prayer that I had never experienced before in my life. In fact, I couldn't wait to pray. I christened my favourite chair my 'prayer chair', and I would head for that. Of course, not being a morning person, I would pray at night—10:30 pm when all the smoke of the day had cleared, the meetings over, and the phone stopped ringing. I gave the Lord 20 minutes a day—big-hearted Al, last of the big-time spenders!

Of course I would get interrupted. The phone would ring occasionally, or somebody would come to the door, or a meeting would go over time. And I couldn't miss my appointment with the 11 o'clock news. That was the extent of my new commitment. But it was more commitment than I had ever had before in my life.

In June of 1975, I went to the priests' retreat in Steubenville. There were about 550 of us attending and a team of four doing the talking and the leading. One of the priests on the team was Father John Randall, and one day he spoke on prayer. I was sitting with my chair tipped back in the very last row. He said all the right things about prayer, and then he said: "Of course, for a priest an hour a day is a minimum." I nearly fell off the chair! I turned to the fellow next to me and asked: "What did he say? How long?" He responded: "an hour, an hour a day."

An hour? Good heavens! The only thing I could think of was the holy hour—the hour that I had barely made it through almost 20 years before.

But before I left Steubenville, I had determined that I would become a morning person. I would set my alarm at a certain time, get up, and spend one hour in prayer every day. And I've done it ever since. In fact, it's more than an hour now. I can't do without it. I don't want to do without it. It's incredibly blessed. Not always easy, sometimes a little dry, but always good. There is a certain gift of prayer, but it starts with the decision.

But before we can go anywhere with this thing, we have to make up our minds that we're going to do it. I would not be without it. I remember the second day after that Holy Spirit seminar back in 1975. Words were jumping off the pages of the breviary. With psalms that I had read a thousand times before, I would stop and gasp: "Wow, is that ever good! What a fantastic and powerful line that is!" Then I would read them again. That's the gift part. Provided we continue to make the decision to take seriously the Lord's call to prayer, he will give us enough gift to get us going and keep us going.

So... for the disciple of Jesus, there has to be a spontaneous and personal and extended time in prayer. Formal prayer is great. The breviary and the Rosary are wonderful. But what we are talking about here is a private and quiet time, a very personal time, a time for just God and me.

I think I can hear some people saying, "I don't know if I could put in a whole hour. How could I possibly fill in the time?"

It's time to get practical. We do need some kind of structure. Jesus implied that when he gave us the Lord's Prayer. There are certain components to prayer, and there are many formats possible. It is good to be flexible and not tied to anything. It's best not to canonize any particular procedure. But I would like to present one possible format as to how the hour could go. It has several components.

1. Thanksgiving

We can begin by giving thanks to God for all things that are good, and in everything else. Not all things that happen in my life are good. They're not all clear blessings. Everyday some good things happen, and some that aren't so good. God does not cause the bad things, but if I thank him in the bad things, he can bring good out of them. *All things work together unto good for those who love God* (Rom 8:28 Douay). I go back over the day, in reverse order, through the previous 24 hours, and I thank the Lord for and in all the events.

The bad stuff is to be embraced as the daily cross. Jesus said, *No one can be my disciple unless he pick up his cross every day and follow along after me* (Luke 14:27 paraphrase). I thank the Lord in it, embrace it, and, with his help, try to carry it. *If you wish to be my disciple,* he said in another place, *you must deny yourself, take up your cross and follow me.* (Matt 16:24 paraphrase). I don't have to go looking for the cross. It will find me.

2. Repentance

If there is anything out of order in my life, I repent. As I go back over the day I say: "I really should have been a little kinder to this person. I really should have been a better listener on that occasion. I really shouldn't have said the other thing. I shouldn't have talked so much. I shouldn't have dominated that conversation. Lord, I don't want to do those things. I would like to be purified. Change my heart." Things like that.

3. Forgiveness

We are to forgive not just because it's a nice thing to do, not just because it's what God does, but because, if we do not forgive, it will hurt us.

I find it hard to go through even one whole day without having somebody step on my toes in one way or other. I have to forgive. I don't have to do it in person. I don't have to write a note. All I've got to do is take him/her in prayer before the Lord and say: "Lord, I forgive so and so."

I'm sure we all have our problems. One of mine is my face. I don't look very lively. So often, people will say to me: "You look tired." Why do people keep telling me I look tired? Don't they know it gets to me? By the time the eighth person in one day tells me I look tired, I feel tired. I do a lot of forgiving.

Are there people in our lives from 10, 20, 50 years ago whom we've never really forgiven? We have to get it over with because it's hurting us. If there is something that happened even many years ago—maybe something our parents did or didn't do, neglected us or didn't pay any attention to us, laid burdens or guilt trips on us—and we've never forgiven them, it has done us harm every day of our lives. It will continue to hurt us until we forgive. When we forgive, we open the door for the Lord to begin to heal the hurts in our lives.

4. Praise

Why should I praise God? He certainly doesn't need it. (In fact, he doesn't need anything). But I need to praise him. If I don't praise God, I will forget who I am. I'll begin to think I'm in charge. I will begin to think that I am God. If I don't praise God, I will begin to think that I am the centre of the universe.

The Lord knows we are supposed to praise him. That is why he urges us to do it. It's the first component of the Lord's Prayer: "Hallowed by thy name." We do it at the beginning of Mass: "Glory to God in the highest." The Church has always prayed that way. We need to give praise to God.

We can praise God alone in our private prayer time, which is what we're talking about here, and we can praise God together.

Praise is the first element of Christian worship. It takes us out of ourselves and it focuses us on God. We are at our finest when we stand in praise of God. It is the most appropriate expression of the relationship between us and God. It is our natural response to God once we perceive him as he is. It is of the essence of heaven. Praise will be ongoing in paradise. We might as well get good at it now.

Praise is not just for extroverts, by the way. Some people say, "Oh well, that's for them. They do all this 'Praise the Lord' stuff because they're so outgoing." We are all supposed to be a people of praise.

We have to use our voices. And this can relate to private prayer as well as prayer together, because we can speak out loud in the privacy of our rooms. *Praise him with full voice* (Tob 13:6). *They raised a mighty clamour before the Lord* (Ezra 3:13 paraphrase). *Shout joyfully to God all the earth... Proclaim his glorious praise* (Ps 66:1-2). *Lift up your voices and glorify the Lord* (Sir 43:31). While they were in jail, *Paul and Silas were praying and singing hymns to God* (Acts 16:25). Using one's voice in praise of God is obviously something the Scriptures endorse, and in faithfulness to the Scriptures the Church has always done so as well.

We should also use music and song. *Strike up the instruments. Sing a new song to our God. Chant to the Lord* (Jdt 16:1). *Sing out with joy. With all the stringed instruments, loudly sing his praises* (Sir 39:15 paraphrase). Stringed instruments, in our day very much in vogue, actually preceded the organ in the whole history of praise among God's people. My own favourite musical instrument is the pipe organ, but the arrival of guitars and the like on the scene a few years ago was not exactly new.

We can use our hands and arms. *All the people, their hands raised high, answered 'Amen. Amen'* (Neh 8:6). *All you people clap your hands. Shout to God with cries of gladness* (Ps 47:2). *Hear the sound of my pleading. I lift my hands towards you*

(Ps 28:2 paraphrase). *Lifting up my hands, I call upon your name* (Ps 63:5). *It is my wish that, in every place, the men should offer prayers with blameless hands held* [*high*] (1 Tim 2:8). He goes on to say: "I don't want any argument about this either." So when we see people clapping their hands in church, they're really not doing something so strange. Some people may not want to do it. That's fine. But it looks as though it's something quite normal for human beings to do. And I have the impression that God likes it.

We might even consider dancing before the Lord. David did it. David danced before the Lord (*cf.* 2 Sam 6:14). I'm not very good at this myself and I don't know what I'd do if people started getting out into the aisles and dancing around during a hymn of praise. I suppose I'd smile and hope that not too many others were being offended. I would also probably try to follow up with a little teaching to straighten things out and put the dancing in some kind of context.

Of course, there is also room for kneeling, bowing, and prostrating before the Lord. *Solomon knelt before the altar, hands outstretched toward heaven* (1 Kgs 8:54 paraphrase). *All the people bowed low, prostrating themselves to the ground*" (Neh 8:6). *Let us bow down in worship* (Ps 95:6). *Paul knelt down with them all and prayed* (Acts 20:36).

I remember officiating at a wedding one time between a Catholic and a Presbyterian in the days when I had to run the rehearsals myself. At one point in the proceedings I suggested, "You can kneel for the blessing." After it was over, the young man came up to me and said: "Would it be alright if we sat for the blessing?" I replied: "It doesn't matter to me. Of course you can sit. Have you a bad knee or something?" "No, Father", he said, "but good Presbyterians don't kneel in church." I responded, "Well, far be it from me to tell good Presbyterians what to do in church." Nevertheless, the Scriptures do allow for kneeling.

5. Invoking the Holy Spirit

As I mentioned previously, every morning I call upon the Holy Spirit: "Holy Spirit reign. Holy Spirit rule. Holy Spirit roll." I invite the Father to stir up the Holy Spirit within me and within this place, and then in Jesus' name I invite the Holy Spirit to do his work, to testify to Jesus and to come against the evil spirits that might be lurking around.

Then I command to depart whatever evil spirits might be thinking of interfering. I often include some of the following uglies: Division, Rebellion, Deception, Confusion, Criticism, Skepticism, Cynicism, Doubt, Disbelief, Worldliness, Materialism, Secularism, Lust, Gluttony, Pride, Anger and Fear. I chase some every morning, but, since I'm often not quite sure if they're getting the message, I put on the full armour of God described in Ephesians 6:13-17. I take the Lord at his Word: *The weapons of our warfare are mighty to the pulling down of the strongholds of the enemy* (2 Cor 10:4 KJV). And I believe Jesus when he says, *I have given you power to tread upon snakes and scorpions* (Luke 10:19).

6. Accepting God's Love

I find it helpful to visualize God, my heavenly Father, ministering his love to me in whatever way I feel I need it.

7. Surrender

I yield over my life, my position, my plans, my priorities, my possessions, my privacy, and whatever else I can think of.

8. Resignation

Have I ever felt that if I don't do such and such, that so and so is not going to get touched by God? And it's got to be me that does it? Well, in fact, it doesn't have to be me at all. And it probably won't be me. Every day I resign as saviour of the world. Sometimes I even write it out and sign my name. I think a lot of parents get into this trap with their children: "If I don't..., then it won't happen." That's not true. Parents are not the saviours of their children. The Lord never appointed any of us as saviour. All we have to do is be faithful to him. He will do the saving.

So I resign. I tell the Lord that I want to get out of his way.

9. Trust

God is very trustworthy. We have every reason to trust God. Esther, in Old Testament times, was sent by the Lord on a perilous mission. She could easily have died. But she said: *"If I perish, I perish"* (Esth 4:16). That's trusting God.

I spoke some very brave words a few years back when I was planning a trip to Medjugorje. At that time, there were shootings in airports, and a number people had said: "There's no way you should go. Aren't you afraid?" My brave little speech was: "If the Lord has more work for me to do, he'll get me back here safely. If he doesn't have any more work for me to do, then there's no point in my coming back." People were very impressed. I'm not sure, however, that my heart matched up with my rhetoric.

There is an incredible story in 2 Maccabees 7. A mother and her seven sons were arrested for not following the false worship of the emperor. They were being threatened with execution. Eventually they were all martyred, one at a time starting with the oldest son, going right down to the youngest—a boy maybe 11 or 12 years old—and then finally the mother. As each one gave up his life, he explained why he would not betray God. Each one had a new insight. The mother watched all of her sons die. She cheered them on. It is an inspiring story and a prime example of trusting in God no matter what.

Psalm 27 puts it very well: *"Though an army encamp against me, my heart will not fear. Though war* [*break out against me*], *even then will I trust"* (Ps 27:3). Can I imagine myself in my armour, with my little dagger, with the enemy, thousands upon thousands of troops—the cavalry, the infantry with the shields and the big swords, the guns, the tanks—all ready to move against me? Would I trust in God then? He wants me to. Even if war break out against me, even then, he wants my trust.

Has anyone ever trusted in the Lord and been disappointed? (Sir 2:10 NABRE). Never! *Blessed is the man who trusts in the Lord. He is like a tree planted beside the waters stretching out its roots* (Jer 17:7-8).

We are to trust in the Lord, especially when things go wrong. I have difficulty with this. It has taken me a long time to learn how to trust God. I'm still not very good at it but I'm improving. Trusting the Lord is not a gift; it is a decision.

10. Scripture

No time of prayer can be complete unless I get the Bible out and ask the Lord for some kind of word for my life. I can ask him where he might want me to look. Or I can follow some kind of plan and pick some passages myself. For example, I can go over the Gospel of St. Matthew and the Acts of the Apostles a few verses at a time. When I get to something that I find strikes a responsive chord in me, I can stop and ask: "Lord, what are you saying to me?"

11. Listening

It's important to fall quiet and listen for awhile. We can say: "Speak, Lord, for your servant is listening. I want to hear what you have to say." It's good to take some time with that.

12. Petition

We must not be afraid, or shy, or ashamed to ask for things. Jesus urges us to ask. In Luke 11, he tells the story of the householder pounding on his neighbour's door. Jesus uses this example to show us that we should continue to ask. If friendship doesn't get him up, persistence will win the day, Jesus explains. And he goes on to tell us that's how to approach the Father. We are to pester him, to stay on his case, to persevere. *Cast your cares upon the Lord, and he will support you* (Ps 55:23).

I find the third chapter of the Book of Tobit particularly significant. Two suppliants, Sarah and Tobit, pray separately. The prayers of these two were *heard in the glorious presence of Almighty God* (Tob 3:16) but there was a delay. The Lord wanted them to persevere, to keep praying. Eventually their prayers would be answered.

And then there is Luke 18, the story of the unjust judge. A widow, a spirited little lady, has a complaint. And the judge, a very worldly man, has no intention whatever of doing her any favours, or even giving her justice. But she persists. And the unjust judge says to his cohorts: *If I don't give this widow what she wants, she will end by bothering me to death* (Luke 18:5 paraphrase). Jesus teaches us to keep praying. He says: *Will he (God) fail to answer, even if he delay* (Luke 18:7 paraphrase)? God's timing is sometimes subtle and elusive. We have to keep at it. We must hang in there.

13. Declaration of Availability

I tell the Lord he can do whatever he wants: "Lord, I don't think I'm qualified for much. I'm not really ready for too many things either—but I'm available. If you want me, here I am. Show me what you want me to do."

14. Waiting

I tell the Lord I will wait upon him, wait for his timing to click in. This isn't easy because his timing and ours are usually very different.

The above 14 phases of prayer are plenty to take any of us through an hour. In fact, the problem will be trying to get them all in under 60 minutes. Most days, we'll probably have to be content just doing some of them.

My 'system' is only one way to go about personal prayer, but it works for me.

The Lord wants communion with us. There is no better time than now to allow this intimacy to begin to happen. We can do it simply by spending time with him as we would with any friend. If someone is my friend I will want to spend time with him/her. It is the same with the Lord. I want to spend some time with him.

He has a capacity that we don't understand, the capacity to be totally preoccupied with each one of us. For him, I am the only person in his life. He's able to do that because he is God. Even the best of fathers with a number of children can't give each one of them total undivided attention. But God, our Father, can do it and will do it if we allow him to.

Just one last little item. I find that some of my best results in prayer come when I complain. Complaining to the Lord is very Scriptural.

When things are not happening, when things are slowing down, when things happen I don't expect to happen, when I get messed up, when I assume God is going to do this and it goes in another direction, then I complain. Here are some verses from the Bible that are worth noting carefully:

O Lord, how long? I am wearied with sighing. (Ps 6:4)
How long, O Lord? Will you utterly forget me? (Ps 13:2)
How long will you hide, Lord? Forever? (Ps 89:47)
Why, Lord, do you stand aloof? In times of distress you hide. (Ps 10:1)
Why do you hide, O Lord? Why do you reject me? (Ps 88:15)
I am wearied with calling. (Ps 69:4)
I am like a broken dish. (Ps 31:13)
I am like some lonely bird on a roof. (Ps 102:8)

I have become like an owl among the ruins. (Ps 102:7)
I moan like a dove. (Isa 38: 14)
If I should dispute with you, O Lord, you would be in the right. Even so, I must discuss this case with you. (Jer 12:1)
How long, O Lord? I cry for help and you do not listen. Destruction and violence are before me, strife and clamourous discord. (Hab 1:2-3)
I will stand at my guardpost, station myself and keep watch to see what he will say, what answer he will give to my complaint. (Hab 2:1)

All of these are from God's own inspired, written Word.

When we get to the point in our pilgrimage with the Lord where we can feel comfortable complaining to him (not angrily; just in a pleading way), we get to a level that is a prelude to our eternal destiny. We are destined to be in an intimate relationship with our God forever. He wants to give us a taste of that now, and that comes as we commit ourselves to regular personal prayer.

Study Questions:

1 In this chapter, Fr. Bob touches on the primacy of prayer. Practically speaking, how might this change the priorities of your daily schedule?

2 Fr. Bob points out that unforgiveness is a serious barrier in one's prayer life: "Jesus talked a lot about forgiveness. In fact, he said there wasn't much point even in trying to pray if there are some unreconciled matters extant."

Are there any barriers of unforgiveness in your own life? Decide to forgive and take a few moments to express a prayer of forgiveness to the Lord.

3 In **The Catholic Disciple** video series, Fr. Bob shared a prayer of surrender that he prayed daily. As a way of surrendering your life more deeply to the Lord, we invite you to make this prayer your own:

Everything I am, everything I have, everything I think, say or do, every vision or dream, every hope for your kingdom, all burdens and trials, every person, every relationship, everything you've done, are doing, and will do, I ascribe them all to you and I give you permission to do today whatever you want to do in my life, in our lives together. Just give me a clue as to what you're doing and I'll support it. Amen.

CHAPTER SEVEN

Wisdom

Wisdom has to do with discerning God's will. In other words:

- What does God want me to do?
- What does he want for my life?
- What does he want for my future?
- What does he want me to be involved in now?
- What does he want my priorities to be?
- What is his will for us as a body of people that have come together and committed themselves not only to the Lord, but to one another as members of a parish?

Just about everybody has prayed for guidance from God at some point in his life. If we think it is good to pray for guidance, then we have to believe that the Lord is ready to guide. And if the Lord is ready to guide, he has to have some way of speaking his word to us. If we pray for guidance, we believe that God will come through for us.

Surprisingly, some people object to this whole notion. They say: "But doesn't the will of God always happen?" Not at all. Not everything is the will of God. There are all kinds of things that happen in this world that are not the will of God at all—war, sickness, illness, even death. Death was never God's idea (*cf.* Wis 1:13).

When the disciples asked Jesus to show them how to pray, one of the first things he taught them to say was: *Your will be done on earth as it is in heaven* (Matt 6:10). Why is Jesus urging us to pray that the Father's will be done? Because it isn't being done, that's why.

This is why we have to seek God's will. If we don't know it, how can we do it?

The will of God is probably a lot more specific than we would ordinarily suspect. The will of God is more than just "do good and avoid evil." It can often be "do this good thing and not those good things."

But we have to be cautious. And sensible. Common sense is one of God's most basic gifts. Tracking down the Lord's will can be overdone. I don't think he is terribly interested in what kind of toothpaste we use. Or when we're going for a drive on a Sunday afternoon, I don't think it matters to him whether we turn to the right or to the left.

Once some people latch onto the reality that the Lord would like to guide them, they begin to see signs all over the place, signs popping up left, right, and centre. It can get out of hand, out of proper perspective. People can be waiting for some concrete sign well beyond the point where God wants them to make a decision. It is without question that he wants to guide us, to give us his wisdom. But it's a hazardous field. Discernment, catching God's wisdom, is critical.

The Lord has a purpose for people's lives. Jesus says it himself. *"The Pharisees and the lawyers, by failing to receive [John's] baptism defeated God's plan in their regard"* (Luke 7:30). So we can defeat the plan of God by not following his will. By not falling into line with his plan, we can miss it. There is a plan for our lives. King Jehosaphat of Judah, wondering whether or not to go into battle, said to those around him: *"Seek the word of the Lord at once"* (1 Kgs 22:5). The Bible is filled with similar references. The Lord has a specific plan and will for us, and he wants us to seek it. As we do, he communicates it to us. As we carry it out, his will gets done on earth as it is in heaven.

Seeking the Lord's will is a standard procedure in the Scriptures. Moses and the Israelites in the desert were led by a cloud by day and a fire by night (Exod 13:21). Whenever the cloud rose, the Israelites would pull up camp and follow. But if it did not lift, they would not go (Exod 40:37). With the cloud by day and the fire by night, the Lord led his people through the wilderness. It's a rather dramatic example. Many might say that we don't have the cloud or the fire anymore. That, of course, is true. But I don't think, at the same time, that we can assume the whole principle, the well documented operational technique of the Lord, no longer applies. The Lord still wants to lead his people. The New Testament continues the experience of the old. Luke writes of the occasion when Barnabas had gone to Tarsus to fetch Saul (Paul) and bring him to Antioch (*cf.* Acts 11:25). Paul had had the powerful experience on the road to Damascus where he was told by the Lord that he would be used powerfully to bring the Gospel to the Gentile world. But the timing was subtle.

Paul had to learn how to wait. We all have to learn the same thing. The Lord has a plan. As St. Luke describes it, as the Christians were gathered 'round celebrating what he calls the 'Liturgy of the Lord', the Holy Spirit spoke within the context of the celebration: *I want Barnabas and Saul set apart for the work that has been [assigned] to them* (Acts 13:2). The word of the Lord, it would seem, was given to them in the context of the liturgy.

I wonder how that worked? It was probably very simple. Someone perhaps said: I feel the Lord may be saying he wants Barnabas and Saul for a particular purpose and mission. The rest of the participants would most likely confirm it. The Lord's word did not likely come as a thunderbolt out of the cloud, but rather into the meeting of the believers as they gathered in faith and in prayer, worshiping God.

God's will was communicated to these people because they were eager to hear it. That's the way it works.

As the story in Acts develops, God's word continues to be available to them. As Paul and his companions head through Asia Minor (modern-day Turkey), they say something like: "Let's go south. That's where the population centres are." But the Holy Spirit wouldn't let them go (*cf.* Acts 16:6).

They tried again: "Let's head north into Bithynia," they might have said: "That seems to be the next logical step." But again the Holy Spirit prevented them. So they waited. Eventually, God's will became clear: they were to go to Macedonia. How would it all happen? Most probably the Lord simply spoke his word in the hearts of those who were gathered together seeking his will. Perhaps one would say: "I don't think the Holy Spirit wants us to go south." Another would reply: "Let's pray about it a little more. Let's wait a bit."

The whole business of seeking God's will is threaded through the Scriptures from beginning to end. Does God really want to convey his will to us, to tell us what to do? Paul says that he has been praying for them that they *attain full knowledge of* [*the Father's*] *will through perfect wisdom and spiritual insight* (Col 1:9). The Lord's 'now word' for us—his direction for our lives—is thus called 'wisdom'.

I recently visited a good friend of mine, Fr. John Randall, in Providence, Rhode Island. His excellent book on the subject is

Wisdom Instructs Her Children. I've learned a lot from him about God's Wisdom.

He tells a story about his working with a body of people, and together seeking the Lord's will. They came once to a point where they weren't sure of a particular decision. They began to seek the Lord. They would meet regularly, and call out for his guidance.

The first time they met, somebody said: "I think what the Lord is saying to us is that we need his wisdom." They all agreed. They sought the Lord for his wisdom. As the weeks went by, they began to realize they didn't know what wisdom was.

"What is wisdom, anyway?" they asked. They began to ask God what it was. "What is this thing we are praying for? What does wisdom really mean?" They persevered in their quest.

Finally, somebody said: "I think the Lord is speaking a very direct word to us about this. I think it's something like this: 'You are asking for wisdom, and you do need it. It is crucial that you have my wisdom, but you are also asking what wisdom is. A good question. I will tell you what wisdom is. Listen to this. Ask me everything. That's wisdom.'"

Although the biblical and traditional concept of God's wisdom is more extensive, a good working definition is just that. It's God's 'now word', his will for me, for us in this particular instance.

Is wisdom important? *The beginning of wisdom is—get wisdom. At the cost of all you have, get understanding* (Prov 4:7). In other words, the smartest thing we can do is find out what God wants and do it.

James 1:5 is reassuring: *If you want wisdom, ask for it.* If we want it, therefore, it's available. We can get it. The Lord wants to convey it to us. Jesus himself operated continually out of the gifts of the Holy Spirit. They have always been present in the Church. St. John Vianney, for example, and St. Catherine of Siena, both had very powerful spiritual gifts of this kind. They knew what was in people's hearts. The Curé told them their sins in Confession before they told him. Catherine of Siena could do the same thing. I know a nun today who has the gift. She can pray with a person and tell him/her the state of his or her heart and soul. She has a special ministry to priests. She calls them to total commitment, total consecration to the Lord. She gives conferences for priests in places near and far.

One time, she was giving a general conference for clergy and others. There was a large turnout. One local priest attended who was very skeptical about her and her gift. He went in sports clothes to be as anonymous as possible and just sat in the crowd to see if there was something he could find to criticize. When she was finished giving her talk, she went down through the crowd, shaking hands with some and saying a prayer with others. When she saw him, she went over and very quietly said: "Father, your heart is not with the Lord." He nearly fainted. It was the beginning for him of a very powerful conversion, a turnaround in his life—a total consecration to the Lord. That's a gift of the Holy Spirit.

Jesus operated continually in these gifts. *The Son does only what he sees the Father doing* (John 5:19 paraphrase).

God's will is the only thing worth doing in life. There is no point in doing anything else. God's will is the only thing that ultimately works anyway. So why do we fight it? Why do we continue to want to do our own thing? Frank Sinatra may have sung; "I did it my way." But that's not God's way. That's the problem with the world. We are doing it our own way. Our way is not always God's way. Somebody should write a song: "I Did It God's Way."

The wisdom of the Lord is not the same as the wisdom of the

world. When worldlings use the word 'wise', they mean something quite different. They are talking about the 'smarts', about being sharp or sage, usually the result of a lot of experience. This is not the wisdom of God.

But his wisdom is available to us. How do we get it? I would like to suggest eight steps. These may seem very simple. Actually they are.

1. We have to understand what wisdom is and believe that the Lord wants to give it to us.

Scripture says this and the Church endorses it. One Christian pastor puts it this way: "I believe the Lord is bombarding the Church with information, but we are not picking it up because we are not looking for it." Father Randall says: "The Lord is on the air." He is like the radio or television stations. But we are not hearing because our receivers are not tuned in. A lot of people say: "I never hear the Lord say anything!" They're not tuned in. It takes a while to get the receiver trained and matured so that it works. That's one of the pitfalls because we get discouraged so quickly. But, if we persevere before the Lord, he'll get through to us.

2. We have to repent.

Repentance is always right near the top of the requirement list for anyone pursuing the Lord. If there is something amiss in my life, there is no way the Lord can get through. If there is something seriously out of order in my life, the Lord is speaking only one word—"Repent." That's the wisdom of God. Once we get repenting, he can start to break through.

3. We have to desire the will of God.

We have actively to want to know what God wants of us, not only believe in it and understand it.

4. We have to ask.

We must not be shy about it. There are a lot of people who don't want to ask God for anything. I think it has to do with the unworthiness that they sense in themselves. One of the biggest problems human beings have is that they don't love themselves.

But God loves us and he must have some reason for it. We must obviously be lovable. Surely, if God can love me, then I can love myself. In fact, I'm offending him when I don't.

But some people have such a deep sense of unworthiness that they can't even approach God and couldn't possibly ask him for anything. But he wants us to ask. Jesus, again and again, encouraged us to ask. Seek the Lord, he said. In fact, pound on his door. Luke 11 and 18 are eminently clear. In both cases Jesus is saying: "Ask. Persevere. Don't give up. Pound on the door. Pound on your Father's door."

5. Abandonment to the will of God.

This is the key. I have to be ready and able to say to God: "Lord, I want to do your will, no matter what it is, even before I know it." Of all the eight steps, this is the most pivotal. This actually stops a lot of people. We're afraid of God.

But God will never ask me to do something without first putting it in my heart. If there is something he wants me to do, but it is not in my heart right now, he will work on me if I let him. If I abandon myself to him, he will change my heart so that I will come to want what he wants. That's the way it works.

I remember one young fellow who had a powerful conversion experience around here when he turned away from the agenda of the world, and gave his whole life to the Lord. I remember talking to him shortly afterwards. He said: "What do I do now Father? How do I grow in my relationship to God?" He was just bubbling over and ready to charge. I thought he was going to tear the place down, brick by brick. I said: "Calm down. That's the first thing to do. Calm down. The second thing to do is to abandon yourself to the will of God. Tell the Lord that you'll do whatever it is he wants." "Oh, yeah, right on! I want to do what God wants. I'll do it." Then he stopped short, "But—what if he wants me to be a priest?" I said, "Well, so what?" "But I don't want to be a priest." So I went through the whole thing of "Is this what the Lord wants for you?" Just tell him that you'll do what he wants. He'll change your heart. You'll want it." He had a lot of trouble with it. But he finally crossed the bar. He did abandon himself to God's will. Shortly after that, the Lord led him to the fine young lady that, in the divine plan, he was to marry. Wedding bells soon sounded and they marched down the aisle. They are now in the process of living happily ever after.

The Lord wants abandonment. He wants us to tell him we will do whatever he wants no matter what it is. That's the key.

6. Listen for God's word in the context of committed relationships.

The will of the Lord is spoken to us much more readily in the context of committed relationships, than when it is just he and I. I find it very difficult to trust a word when a person has heard it all by himself/herself from God. And one of the problems I find with some people is that they seem so sure they are right. That scares me.

We must not be certain that we are right, because, we have to admit it, we can be wrong. Very often, some of the people who claim to catch this sort of individual word from the Lord can actually be very dangerous. They make me very uneasy.

If a word is spoken with great assurance, especially if it has a grain or two of clear truth in it, whether it is from God or not, it can get swallowed whole. Committed relationships bring more people into the picture and can obviate the difficulty.

7. We have to wait.

If abandonment is the key step, waiting is the toughest. Once we tell the Lord to go ahead and do whatever he wants, we must commit ourselves to waiting for him. Perseverance. We must keep knocking on the door. We'll soon learn that God's timing and ours are often very different.

One of the words I thought the Lord was speaking to me, and to the body of young men, that eventually became The Companions of the Cross, went something like this: "I want you to become skilled at waiting for me." Waiting sounds like such a simple thing, but actually it's very, very difficult. We want to get charging forward while the Lord is saying: "Wait."

We cannot ask the Lord for the gift of waiting. It's not a gift. It's a decision. As we decide again and again, day after day, to wait upon the Lord, we get better at it. I'm still not good at waiting upon the Lord, but I'm better at it now than I used to be.

The Lord is very accomplished at waiting. Of course, he's got more time. For millions of years he watched the dinosaurs chew on grass, while he waited to create us. He is good at waiting. We're not. But even though we're not good at it, we still have to do it. We have to wait upon the Lord.

How about a couple of scriptures? *"Leave it to the Lord, and wait for him"* (Ps 37:7). *Will the Lord refuse to hear even if he delay in answering?* (Luke 18:7 paraphrase). Luke records the parable of the persistent widow and the unjust judge. We simply have to wait it out.

Let's wait, for heaven's sake. Let us not make the decision until somehow we get a notion that the Lord has said something. Then we can do it. Until then, we wait. We wait upon the Lord.

Write the vision down clearly on tablets so that all can read and understand. It will surely come. It has its time. Even if it delays, wait for it (Hab 2:2-3 paraphrase). If abandonment to the Lord is the key step, waiting is the most difficult of them.

And we can get so tired waiting. I remember a few years ago saying: "Lord, why can't you move faster? Why are you so slow? I know you've got all kinds of time, but I don't." I've lived to eat those words several times. Very often, I have had to run to catch up. I've heard myself say: "Wait a minute, Lord. Not so fast!" When the God starts to do things, he can move very quickly. We may think time is running out. Then the Lord starts to move. First thing we know, it's all done. If we're not waiting and watching, we're going to miss it.

8. Test it out.

When we think we have a sense of what the Lord might be saying, we test it out. We give it a shot. We see what happens. We can't be afraid to make mistakes.

We can't be so sure we have it right. We have to wait to see what follows.

We have to take God very seriously, but we must not take ourselves too seriously. We have to have the kind of humour or balance whereby we can laugh at ourselves, and allow ourselves to get it wrong sometimes. We will find getting it wrong at times is part of the way that God teaches us how to get it right. We learn from our mistakes.

How does God's wisdom come? Most often it comes as a sense of peace in my heart. That's not the same as feeling good, by the way.

For example, in the summer of 1984, while I was giving talks in different places, I sensed the Lord was saying to me that he wanted me to go home in September, sit down and keep quiet, and listen for a while, because he was going to change my program. I didn't know if that was for real. I bounced it off people with whom I was in relationship and they said: "It sounds pretty good." So I obeyed, and within days after I got home in September, I sat down and kept quiet. I was quickly and unexpectedly appointed pastor of St. Mary's parish. It was unlikely because appointments are not made in September. They are made in June. It was a total surprise for me. And yet it confirmed the word of wisdom that I believed the Lord had given me during the summer.

Another example. When I got to St. Mary's in the fall of 1984, I said: "Lord, what am I supposed to do? I've never done this before!" I sensed the Lord was saying: "Give me permission. I want permission to do what I want to do here. I want you to step out of the way. Never mind your programs and your bright ideas. You step out of the way and let me take over. Then you can stand up and tell the people you are doing it, and tell them I want their permission, too." I was terribly embarrassed doing that. I thought I was going to sound ridiculous. "Lord, I'm going to look silly," I said. It was almost as though the Lord were saying: "But you've looked silly for years. What have you got to lose?" I was peaceful about the business of coming home and keeping quiet, but I didn't feel particularly good about it. I was peaceful about the notion of saying: "I give you permission." At the same time, I didn't feel very good about that either. I felt awkward, in fact. So peace in my heart is not the same thing as feeling good, not the same at all. It is a deep reality that takes hold in my heart and my spirit. It is called God's peace.

Relying on God's wisdom brings us into a whole new mind set, probably related to what St. Paul meant by the renewal of the mind: *Do not conform yourselves to this age, but be transformed by the renewal of your mind, so that you may judge what is God's will* (Rom 12:2). It's a renewal of our minds that we need, to believe that God has a plan and is ready to speak it. It's an adventure jumping into the whole pursuit of God's will. It's exciting, challenging, sometimes exhausting, sometimes frustrating, but always good. It is a whole renewal of the mind, a different way of thinking. It's a spiritual way of thinking as St. Paul says: *Acquire a fresh, spiritual way of thinking* (Eph 4:23).

Seeking the wisdom of the Lord and operating out of it is a whole different type of thing. When we tell people who do not believe the Lord does things like that, they will think we are crazy. A lot of people think I am crazy, in fact. I used to be so dependable. I used to have such a good reputation. Around Ottawa, I used to be considered as solid as a rock, actually called by some 'the Rock of Gibraltar'. Now I'm a real nut case. I say: "Lord, why is this? What have you done to me? Could I not have a shred of reputation left?" It's as though the Lord is saying: "Well, Jesus didn't get a very good press, either. Don't worry about it."

A whole new ministry principle for me is to see what God is doing and minister to that. Where is the Lord doing something? There are thousands of good ideas we can try to implement. There are hundreds and hundreds of good works for God we could undertake. We can do this, do that, galvanize, organize, capitalize all kinds of stuff. But if it's not what God is saying, all we're going to do is burn out, get frustrated and fed up with the whole thing. But when we operate out of the wisdom of God, we see what the Lord is doing and it drives us on.

People say: "I've tried Father. I've tried. I've tried this. I've tried that. What do I do?" I say: "Calm down." One of the things you might consider is looking around and seeing what God is doing in your community. Where is the Lord at work? When you see something you think he's doing, go and do it with him. Go and join up with that, and do it and seek the Lord's will for you. Don't get all burnt-out and bent out of shape trying to do good things for God that he is not telling you to do. It won't work.

We're not supposed to do good things. We're to do God's thing.

Sometimes people say: "Well, what am I supposed to do—just

sit in a corner and wait for God to give me some kind of signal?" No, that's not it at all. Waiting for the Lord does not mean standing still. Waiting for the Lord means moving forward at our regular pace doing the obvious thing. There are duties we have every day. We have to get up in the morning for one thing. We have to pray. We have to talk to people. We have to keep moving forward while giving the Lord leave to convey his will. He will catch up with us somewhere along the way.

The Lord's word to me usually doesn't come while I am sitting quietly in prayer. It usually comes to me when I am going forward during the day. Sometimes, when I am talking to somebody I have the sense that the Lord is speaking to me and I wind up saying something I never thought of, something that had never before occurred to me. Yet here I am saying it. I find very often that's the way he deals with me. It can be different for different people. But waiting for the Lord does not mean sitting in a corner, or standing still and going nowhere.

Waiting for the Lord requires a childlike trust. Jesus says: *I assure you, unless you change and become like little children, you will not enter the Kingdom of God* (Matt 18:3). Children do not assume they know very much. Therefore, they ask a lot of questions. I think that's what Jesus means. We must not assume we know very much. We have to ask the Lord a lot of questions, as in Fr. Randall's example: "Ask me everything." The Lord is ready to lead. Otherwise, we can thrash around with a thousand and one good ideas and get nowhere.

When the Lord gives the direction and we do it, he supplies the power. When he makes the order, he writes the cheque. He underwrites everything he directs. We have to rely on the power of God. And we need his wisdom.

The people perish for want of a vision (Prov 29:18 paraphrase). "Vision" means a direction, some word from the Lord about where to go and how to get there. People perish for want of it.

We get so stuck when we don't have a sense of where the Lord wants to lead us. *The Lord does nothing without [first] revealing his plan to his servants, the prophets* (Amos 3:7). We need to trust, as we come together as a body of people, that the Lord will speak his word, and that somehow in our midst, the word can be caught. Maybe somebody among us is better than most at catching the word. That is the gift of prophecy. We have to look for it and wait upon it.

When we allow God to move, he does. He is eager to direct. He is looking for willing people. *The eyes of the Lord range across the whole of the earth searching out those who are wholehearted for him, so that he might encourage them* (2 Chr 16:9 paraphrase). We want to be "wholehearted" for the Lord, so that he can encourage us by showing us what he wants us to do, and by giving us the power to carry it out.

When we open the door, the Lord enters. Things happen, sometimes unexpectedly, very often things we would not choose. Sometimes in trying to follow the Lord, we get into a type of pleasant chaos. This is OK. The chaos is a result of our own plans breaking down. We must not get upset by it. Sometimes the Lord allows a little chaos as he takes charge and speaks his word into a people's midst so that they can catch it and move with him. A kind of peaceful confusion can reign for a little while. We are never sure where he is going to take us next.

When we find out what the Lord's plans are and carry them out, they work.

It is exciting to think that God actually has plans for me personally, for my family, my parish, the body of people I belong to. It's exciting. It's eminently worth pursuing. In fact, I cannot imagine anything more worth doing than pursuing the Lord's plans. We must not get discouraged by the mistakes that we make. That's part of the learning process.

St. Paul writes: *I have been praying for you unceasingly, and asking that you may attain full knowledge of his will through perfect wisdom and spiritual insight* (Col 1:9). And notice what else he says: *Then you will lead a life worthy of the Lord, pleasing to him in every way. You will multiply good works of every sort* (Col 1:10). With the Lord's direction, with his wisdom, it will work. His Kingdom will get built the way he wants it built. My ideas will go on the shelf. My priorities will be set aside. My agenda will be written off. If we give up writing the script for God, he writes it. That's much better.

Study Questions:

1 *Do not be conformed to this world but be transformed by the renewal of your mind, that you may prove what is the will of God, what is good and acceptable and perfect* (Rom 12:2). Fr. Bob comments, "It's a renewal of our minds that we need, to believe that God has a plan and is ready to speak it... [It's] a different way of thinking... It's a spiritual way of thinking."

Why is this transformative "way of thinking" so important for discernment?

2 *The Lord does nothing without first revealing his plan to his servants, the prophets* (Amos 3:7). Fr. Bob comments, "[Therefore] we need to trust, as we come together as a body of people, that the Lord will speak his word, and that somehow in our midst, the word can be caught."

Have you ever experienced this? Describe some practical ways to look for and wait upon the Lord's 'now word'.

3 Think of a situation or decision in your life where you need God's wisdom. Try using the following steps of discernment to discover God's plan:

1 Understand what wisdom is
and believe that God wants to give it to you.

2 Repent.

3 Desire the will of God.

4 Ask God.

5 Abandon yourself to the will of God.

6 Listen for God's word in the context
of committed relationships.

7 Wait.

8 Test it out.

CHAPTER EIGHT

Healing

A whole person is one who is perfect. It is God's plan that we enter into wholeness. Woundedness is not his idea. Wholeness is. The Lord's plan for us is that we enter into friendship with him. We are called into friendship with the awesome Father of us all, with Jesus, the eternal Saviour, and with the Holy Spirit of incredible wisdom, strength and power. It's amazing to think of it, but the Lord wants intimacy with us.

The Lord doesn't need us but "God is love," as St. John says. Love, being what it is, has the desire to share. We are the results of God's desire to share his life. The Father wants a larger family—not that the Father, the Son and the Holy Spirit aren't enough in their perfect Trinity—but the Lord wants us to be part of that. He wants to get involved with us. He has made us free. As Pope John Paul II said a few years ago: "Our basic problem is freedom (I thought he was going to say sin) because being free we can choose less than what God offers." That's sin, and that, of course, is our problem.

Some people have said: "If only we weren't free to sin, then we wouldn't have all these problems and we could enter into a fullness of life with God forever." In fact, we could not, because, in order to share God's life, we have to be like him, and he is free. The Lord entices us to make a free choice for him. Human life on earth isn't about the stock market, business, international politics, intrigue, holidays, or wealth. The basic purpose of life is to hear the invitation of God to eternal life and to say "Yes" to it, embrace it, and live it out.

The Kingdom of God exists when the will of the Father is done completely and fully. In heaven, God's will is always done perfectly. Heaven is co-terminus with the Kingdom of God. But that is not the case on earth. It is the Holy Spirit's task to bring forth the Kingdom of God on earth as it is in heaven. It is the Lord's intention to endow us with life to the full. In order to do that he has to heal us to perfection.

Our problem is sin. The weight of human sin presses down upon human society. When Jesus came to earth (the name Jesus means 'God saves'), he came to save us from our real problem—sin. Sin is the root cause of all our other problems. For example, Jesus didn't come to save his people from the Roman overlords, but the reason they were under foreign domination was because of their sinfulness. He didn't come to create Shangri-La on earth, but to deliver us from sin.

"If God is good, why is the world in such a mess?" It's an often-asked question. Have we ever noticed that this is a theoretical question for us only until some kind of sorrow or tragedy enters into our lives? Then the question becomes: "If God is good, how could this terrible evil thing have happened to me?" The answer to both these questions is the same: It has come about because of the weight of sin that presses down upon the whole of human society. All evils are explainable through that. It isn't related to my own sin, but to the combined sin of mankind. God didn't make the world in bad shape. But we have managed to do that. We have taken control away from God. Instead of running the world God's way, we do it by politics, plebiscite, and popular will.

Right now, the abortion issue is front and centre—the right to life versus the right, as it is called, to choose. What will the ultimate decision be based upon? It will be based upon public opinion, won't it? We have taken charge of God's creation. At this moment in our country, we have no abortion law whatsoever. No doubt, we will soon pass one which will allow the taking of human life under certain conditions, and we'll figure: "Sure, we've compromised, but we've got somewhere." We've got nowhere! As citizens of this country, every one of us is going to have to pay the price for the grievous sin of abortion.

A priest whom I respect very much said a few years ago: "Abortion is the father of the coming nuclear holocaust." Some might say that's a very pessimistic view. Hopefully, we can avoid the nuclear holocaust, but allowing abortion is simply moving us toward it. It offends the whole way that God has created us. We are tampering seriously with God's law. When we do that, things tend to come apart. The world is in such a mess because we have contrived to make it that way.

Some people claim that God's will is always done. God's will is for life to the full. Wholeness is his plan. God's will is not being done, and that is why Jesus urges us to pray: "Thy will be done."

There are different kinds of healing. It can be physical, spiritual, emotional, or psychological. Although different, they are all related to what God wants to do.

As far as affliction or illness or disease are concerned, Jesus made only one response. When he came across somebody who was sick, he didn't say: "You have to offer up your sufferings." His only approach to human sickness was to heal it. There were times when he went to his home town of Nazareth and couldn't perform any miracles there because of the citizens' lack of faith. The same thing happened at Capernaum, the town he made his base of operations. The power of the Holy Spirit flowed through Jesus undoing the damage done by sin. If I am ill, it is because I live in a sinful world. If I am healed by the power of God, it is because the Lord has broken through and touched me.

Jesus healed a blind man at Bethsaida (*cf.* Mark 8:22-26). He led him outside town. There he prayed for him, touched his eyes, and asked him: "Can you see now?" "I can see things I've never seen before, but I can't see very clearly," he answered. "What I think are people, look like trees walking around." Jesus prayed for him again, but, we suspect, not without first leading him farther out of town. Then he touched his eyes and asked: "How about now?" The man responded, "I can see perfectly now." Jesus had to create a little space of faith in order for the Holy Spirit to break through the human sinful condition in order to accomplish the healing. That's why Jesus consistently called for repentance. If we want to move towards healing, the first step is always to move away from sin.

Healing and wholeness can get to be a complicated topic. We have to be clear on the role of human remedies as well. We are not talking about setting medical expertise aside, but rather a healing program which includes the medical profession, a field which very often leaves out the Lord. It is important to understand that all healing comes from God, whether it is ministered through prayer or through a physician. Man has not invented remedies. We have only discovered them.

The Book of Sirach has important things to say about medicine: *Hold the physician in honour, for he is essential to you, and God it was who established his profession* (Sir 38:1). *God makes the earth yield healing herbs which the prudent man should not neglect* (Sir 38:4). *When you are ill, delay not, but pray to God, who will heal you* (Sir 38:9). [*The physician*] *beseeches God that his diagnosis be correct and his treatment bring about a cure* (Sir 38:14). So... *Give the doctor his place* (Sir 38:12).

When we've had to go to the doctor for some pain or ache or condition, did we ever think of praying for the doctor? We should try praying that his diagnosis will be correct and that the medication that he prescribes will have no side effects.

In 1988, I had a call from a mother in St. Mary's Parish with five children who said that her three-year-old boy was really sick. It was the typical flu—high fever, no appetite. The boy was in pain and was crying. (I'm told that when I was a child, my temperature used to go through the roof at the slightest provocation. My uncle, the doctor, used to tell my mother: "That's the way children are. Don't worry about it." She worried anyway. She worried me back to health.) "Would you pray for him?" she asked. "Of course," I said, "but pray for him yourself, too. Go over to him right now, put your hands on him and say a prayer. Pray for him again before he goes to sleep tonight, and pray for him tomorrow morning when he wakes up. And continue to give him whatever he is supposed to have." (When I get the flu. my doctor tells me to drink chicken soup. That's it. "Take it easy, drink chicken soup, and rest." I think he's just humouring me. I think the flu is just one of those things we have to endure.)

She called me back later in the day: "I did what you said—I put my hands on him and prayed for healing—and then I went out to the kitchen. Within two minutes, I heard his voice, 'Mummy. Can I have a peanut butter sandwich.' I went back in and felt his forehead. He had no temperature at all. It was gone, just like that."

The skeptic will say: "But that's the way children are. Temperatures can shoot up and down." True, but my problem with that type of skepticism is how so much of that kind of thing seems to happen after we pray.

Jesus has to consistently break through the hold that sin has upon us. In Luke 13:11, Jesus encountered a woman with a severe arthritic condition. She was bent over. He touched her, told her to straighten up, and she did. He said of her condition that she had been held in bondage by Satan for eighteen years. What did he mean? Illness is linked to sin and is the work of the enemy. So the first step towards wholeness and healing is repentance.

Sin is our downfall. The nation of Judah was carried off to captivity to Babylon because of its rebellion, not against Babylon, but against God. *The earth is polluted because of its inhabitants.* [*We*] *have transgressed the law... and a curse devours the earth. Its inhabitants* [*must*] *pay* (Isa 24:5-6). *Its rebellion will weigh it down* (Isa 24:20).

Sin is the root cause of our distress. Violence, hunger, crime, and war—all exist because of the weight of sin. If tomorrow morning at the crack of dawn, the entire human race were to repent of its sinfulness and come into God's will, things would change dramatically.

The hands of God are tied by human sinfulness because he has chosen to abide by our free choices. He will not violate our freedom. When we pray, it is as though we poke holes in the cloud of sin over the human race, and pierce through to the throne of God. As a result of this, his hands become a little freer to move, and he can reach down and touch us. These healings become the signs of which Jesus has spoken.

It is difficult to turn to a page of the Gospels without reading about Jesus touching and healing someone. Everywhere he went, he healed the sick. In some places, they were all healed; in other places he couldn't do a great deal because of their lack of faith. *Those who follow me,* said Jesus, *will be marked by certain identifiable characteristics. One of these will be that they will lay their hands upon the sick and the sick will recover* (Mark 16:17-18 paraphrase). Jesus is saying, in other words: "What I did, you too will do."

As a body of believers, we have to believe that the Lord will touch and heal the sick. We have to be a people who are ready to pray for the sick that they might be healed. Too often we honour that with lip service only. "That's very nice," we say. We believe it, but we don't do it. The early Church experienced it: *Many signs and wonders were done through the apostles* (Acts 2:43 NABRE). *Through the hands of the apostles, many signs and wonders occurred among the people* (Acts 5:12). *He confirmed the message with his grace and caused signs and wonders to be done at their [Paul's and Barnabas'] hands* (Acts 14:3). *Is anyone sick among you? Let him call in the elders of the Church. Let them pray over the sick person and anoint him with oil in the Lord's name. If any sins have been committed, these will be forgiven and health will be restored* (Jas 5:14-15 paraphrase).

The healings that we experience in a physical way will not heal us to immortality. At some point, we still must die and pass through the gates of death. They are simply signs. The Lord blesses us with these signs and wonders for a number of reasons:

1. They are signs of God's love and concern. The Lord loves us. When someone is healed of a physical ailment through beseeching the Lord, the love of God must break through. The Lord must care for me if he's willing to do this.

2. They are signs of his plan. God's ultimate intention is for all of us to be whole and complete. In heaven, we will have perfect glorious bodies, not bodies of flesh, such as we have now, but real bodies, nonetheless. We will recognize others, and they will recognize us.

3. They are signs of the authenticity of the Word. If we are teaching the Word of God authentically, we should expect that God will confirm the Word with signs and wonders.

4. They are signs for unbelievers. Signs are intended by the Lord to turn the hearts of skeptics to God. When Jesus healed the sick, some of the people who saw, believed. When he raised Lazarus from the dead (John 11), many came to believe in him. No wonder. If I'd been there as a skeptic, I think I probably would have been convinced about what Jesus was doing and saying. Strangely enough, not everyone was convinced.

5. Signs can shore up a wavering faith.

6. Signs can encourage the believer. They can build up the ones who already believe. Every time I see some kind of healing, my own faith deepens. Even if no one was ever healed, I would still believe from now to eternity, but signs do strengthen my faith.

What are we supposed to do? We are supposed to believe the Word of God. We are supposed to pray in Jesus' name to the Father. We are to persevere together. Sometimes it works. A lot of times it doesn't. To me the healing ministry of the Church is a mystery. I don't understand why sometimes people get healed and at other times they don't. I've seen all kinds of healings. Has the Lord done any here at St. Mary's? Yes, we've had a fair number of healings right here. They are not dramatic things that made the front page of the paper, or even the back page for that matter, but we've had a number of people touched and healed physically here.

We pray for people all the time. Most of the needs are physical.

We prayed for a fellow suffering from an extremely painful condition called sciatica. The ailment has been healed. He says it has given him tremendous relief. He's sleeping better now than he's slept in years.

An older woman who lives down the street from the church had pain throughout her body. All her bones ached. She couldn't sleep at night, could hardly move, and was continually focused in on the aches and pains. I had never seen her smile. One Saturday afternoon her husband fairly dragged her to the church. I can still see her struggling in the side door. She barely made it to the second row and sat very still during Mass. After Mass, she came up for prayer. At the 9:00 a.m. Mass the next day, I was at the back of the church getting ready to begin. I looked up to see her coming through the door. I said to myself: "Good heavens—she's smiling!" After Mass she came over to me and said: "All the pain is gone." Fantastic!

Earlier there was another woman who had dropped a heavy iron weight on her foot. Her foot was black and blue and she had to limp to church. She came up to Communion hanging onto the pews. As soon as the Sacred Host was placed upon her tongue, the pain went away. She walked back to her seat. Afterwards she met me.

> "I'm confused," she said. "I don't know what to make of what has happened."
>
> "What do you mean?" I asked.
>
> "As soon as I received Communion," she said, "all the pain went away."
>
> "It looks as though the Lord has healed you," I replied.
>
> "I've never heard of such a thing," she responded.
>
> "Well, I have," I had to say, "lots of times."
>
> "I feel so good I think I can take my three children to the closing of the Winterlude this afternoon," she enthused. And she did. She and the children skated on the canal together.

A few years ago, a little boy nine or ten years old who was suffering from asthma and allergies came up to Communion. The minute he drank the Precious Blood from the chalice, all the symptoms disappeared. He went back to kneel beside his father and said, "Daddy, look. My eyes don't hurt anymore." They were clear and he was breathing easily.

At St. Mary's the Lord is confirming his Word with what seem to us to be little signs. They're not making any headlines, but for the people being healed they are big signs. We need to be a people who expect the healing touch of God.

The healing ministry of the Church must go on. Of the three types of healing, physical healings are the easiest to perform and to see, although, strangely enough, they are the ones we expect the least. Spiritual healing is the most powerful because in a spiritual healing what takes place is the conversion of a human heart. It's the most powerful work of God. It is more difficult for a person to be converted to the Lord than it is for a physical body to be healed.

Emotional healings are the most exhausting of the healings to pray for. For example, to heal someone like the good woman down the street who had pain throughout her body, the prayer lasted maybe fifteen seconds, to anoint her took another four or five seconds, and to wish her well, a few seconds more. That's all pretty easy and there's not much to it. Of course, it is the power of God that does this. To see someone through the healing of an emotional problem can be long and difficult. It can go on and on and on, until we are ready to surrender. From the human point of view, it is the most demanding.

In the Liturgy of the Eucharist, we pray specifically for healing. Right after the Our Father, the celebrant prays that the Lord will free us from all anxiety. Anxiety covers a whole multitude of problems. "This is the Lamb of God..." the celebrant says, and we all respond, "Lord, I am not worthy to receive you, but only say the word and I shall be healed." The teaching Church urges us to pray continually for healing. "This is not something reserved for a tent meeting," said a priest one time. "Healings are supposed to happen in the pews and aisles of the church." And one of the little prayers that the priest says quietly before Communion is, "Lord Jesus Christ, with faith in your love and mercy I eat your body and drink your blood. Let it not bring me condemnation, but health in mind and body."[5]

---

5 In the present English translation of *The Roman Missal* [Third Edition, 2011] the celebrant says, "Behold the Lamb of God..." and the people respond, "Lord, I am not worthy that you should enter under my roof, but only say the word and my soul shall be healed." In preparation for Communion, the priest says quietly, "May the receiving of your Body and Blood, Lord Jesus Christ... be for me protection in mind and body and a healing remedy."

The healing of the emotions, the healing of the inner person is sometimes called inner healing, or the healing of memories. This is different from physical healing. This type of healing doesn't have to deteriorate; this is a healing unto perfect wholeness. Our bodies have to suffer and eventually die in order for us to enter into eternity, but in this type of healing, the inner person can simply grow. There doesn't have to be any death to this, in other words. St. Paul writes: *I pray that the Lord will bestow gifts upon you, that your inner self may grow strong through the working of the Holy Spirit* (Eph 3:16 paraphrase). Jean Vanier has said: "The things that we have been through have shaped us and made us into the people that we are. Our present emotional difficulties stem from past experiences—deprivations and traumas, mostly."

If we've ever been deprived of anything, or if we ever endured a trauma—minor or major—it has scarred us. The younger we were when those things happened, the deeper the scars. These wounds can manifest themselves as problems in adult life. Our present difficulties stem from our past experiences.

Children have a great many needs. They need to be secure. They have to know that they are loved. Sensing that they are not wanted can have a very bad effect upon them. Children need to know their limits. They have to know what they're allowed to do. They need affection, love, and discipline from both father and mother, or from good substitutes. Children need affection, need to be touched, need to sit on laps, stuff like that. They need to be respected and trusted. They need a certain amount of freedom. A ten-year-old needs more freedom than a five-year-old; a fifteen-year-old needs more freedom still. They need wise parents that can gradually lead them into that freedom and allow them to discover what it really means. They need the company of other children. They need to stand on their own, to be respected for who they are. The reality is that very often the father or the mother is not there, and without some kind of substitute, children can be damaged.

Youngsters can be hurt if compared with others in an unloving way. I taught high school for a number of years and I came into contact with a lot of this kind of stuff, like the second child whose older brother was an academic whiz, but he wasn't. He just didn't have the same mental makeup and was continually being compared to the older brother. "What's the matter with you? Why can't you do as well as your brother (or the guy next door, or your cousin)? Are you stupid or something? Why are you always dropping things on the floor? Why did you spill the milk like that? You're so clumsy!"

Adults are imperfect and can be wounded too. We bring to our marriages the wounds that we ourselves have, and when we talk sharply to our children and put them down, they become wounded in turn. As a child, if I was talked down to, if I was compared to somebody else, if I was criticized, if I was called names, particularly by my parents, but by other people too, I was hurt. I was wounded inside. These things festered and hung around inside until I was older and then they started to appear in all kinds of unhealthy behaviour patterns. If I am now a parent, I have to be careful how I talk to my children or what I expect of them. If I beat them, they are not only being physically wounded, they are receiving deep emotional scars. If they have fearful experiences, such as seeing someone die or experiencing near-death themselves, this adds to their emotional woundedness. If a child gets up in front of the class to recite a poem and forgets it, and everybody laughs, that child is wounded. If children are accused of things unjustly, it has a scarring effect. Things happen in the little souls that affect their emotional makeup.

When I was teaching boys in school, I was in the Guidance Department and offered individual counselling. The boys would come and invariably the opening statement would be about geography or mathematics, or some other subject. I knew geography wasn't the real problem. Eventually, if I could lead them along a little bit and they could begin to trust me they would open up and we could get to the real problem. The latter so often stemmed from the boy's relationship with his father.

> "I don't get along with my father."
> "I don't like my father."
> "My father doesn't like me."

Father, father, father. I came to the conclusion that we have a severe social problem here. There are some wonderful exceptions, but the general situation is that children are not getting fathered very well. It's tragic. Mothers are stepping in to try to take over from what the fathers are supposed to be doing, but great though they be, they are not ordinarily equipped to be father-substitutes.

All of this is affecting people, and later in life it manifests itself in symptoms like fear of heights or water or crowds, insecurities, anxieties, compulsions, hang-ups, fixations, nervousness, shyness, lack of confidence, instability, sexual difficulty, oversensitivity, hatred, bitterness, depression, poor self-image, anger (there is anger seething inside a lot of people and it comes out at different times in many different ways), overeating, overdrinking, cynicism, people with a short fuse, those that can't make friends. Where do all our adult problems come from? Most of them come from the past. We are the composite of what we've been through.

How do we get free from these things? The behavioural sciences help, but in my experience, the Lord is the one who does the real job of healing. This healing is accomplished through prayer for the healing of memories and is based upon God's omnipresence. The Lord does not have our limitations with regard to space. He is not threatened by the discovery of a new sun that is ten trillion times brighter than our own. He created it! He doesn't have limitations with regard to time either. We don't understand this because we relate only to time and space. We can't go back into the past; it's finished. We can only remember it. We can't see into the future. We can only surmise. We are here, right now. We can go only from one instant to the next. God doesn't have that limitation and we can't understand that. There's no point in even trying. God is God. He is sovereign. He is unlimited.

The natural healing process of an emotional difficulty is gradual. (That is, unless the Lord breaks through all of a sudden). It takes time to heal these things in the same way that psychological counselling takes time. That applies in the physical realm too. For example, if somebody breaks an arm, it is put in a cast, and the natural healing process begins immediately—the bone begins to knit and put itself back together. Why? Because God has placed within the human system the natural healing process. We didn't invent that. We discovered it. God invented it. By the way, if, in that healing process of the arm, we gather round every day and pray, it will heal faster. The same thing applies in the healing of the inner person. If prayer is added to the recalling of the past, then the healing will happen faster. Even so, it is a gradual process. It takes time and, therefore, can be exhausting.

Many different healing techniques have been taught by the prompting of the Holy Spirit within the experience of the Church. Being wounded emotionally may make it difficult to make decisions, for example. It's a real trial to be indecisive because there are a lot of decisions we must make in our day-to-day lives. If we can get into our past with the Lord's assistance and find out the origin of the problem and invite the Lord into that, he can begin to heal the situation.

All this was very new to me until the mid-seventies; in fact, I had never even heard of it. But I began to read about it and found it passably interesting. One night I was invited to join a team of people who were going to pray for a woman who had some emotional problems. I didn't know anything about it, but I was invited to come along so that I might learn something. "Come and just pray quietly," I was told, "and offer your support to what we do."

The situation was this: The woman we were to pray for was in her mid-thirties, with a husband and three children. The family was in reasonably good shape. The children weren't bad, just a little hyperactive. But a problem was beginning to surface in her life that none of them could handle. She was waking up screaming in the middle of the night. She was having a nightmare that would recur night after night. The whole family was beginning to disintegrate. Here was mummy—the one who is supposed to hold the home together—falling apart. What was happening to the good mother here? Nobody knew. We were off to pray for her.

There were five of us—the woman who had the problem, the team of three, and myself, the excess baggage. The whole thing took about 35 minutes. That was fast. Normally inner healing takes much longer, several sessions sometimes. One of the team, a woman, seemed to be the leader and she began to lead the prayer. She began to pray for the present, then back to the birth of the youngest child, the birth of the second child, the birth of the first child, the first few months of marriage, the marriage itself, the courtship. I began to catch on to what she was doing. She was praying through all the potentially traumatic periods of this woman's life and at each step along the way she was inviting the Lord himself to be there. "Be present, Lord, to this young lady as she comes to be married. Take her by the hand and assure her that this is the right decision."

We went backwards into her life, inviting the Lord into every stage along the way—to the time she left school and went to work, then her teenage years, puberty, back to the time she was five or six years of age and starting school. The different members of the three person team would pass the ball one to the other. One would seem to run out of things to pray for and another one would take over. I sat there, like a dummy, not making a sound but quietly praying: "Lord, I know you know what you're doing here and I haven't got a clue, but I hope something good can happen to this fine woman."

When we arrived at the point in her life when the girl was five or six, the team leader began to pray this way: "Dear Father, be present to this little child. Call her by name. (The Father is then right back there with her. He doesn't have the limitations of time that we have.) Gather her in your arms, and hold her close to yourself and assure her that those bombs which are exploding and those planes flying overhead are not going to hurt her." When I heard that I thought: "It's obvious she knows something I don't." We finished by going back through infancy, birth, the time in womb, conception, and ended with a prayer for the parents—all in about 35 minutes.

When the planes and the bombs had been mentioned, the one being prayed for showed just a little emotion, a tear down her cheek. That's all, no big deal, just that. When it was all over, the woman who had been prayed for said: "You know," turning to the team leader, "when you mentioned the planes and bombs, it all came back to me." And then she told us her story. She had grown up in Holland during the war. When she was five or six, the town that she lived in came under nightly bombardment. Every night the sirens would sound, and the parents would gather up the children and head down into the shelters. One night this little girl got lost. The mother had two younger children. The father was away in the Dutch army, and this little child got left behind. She wandered the streets throughout the entire air raid. The child was severely traumatized. The mother dealt with it poorly. She told the girl to forget it, that it would never happen again. "Auntie so-and-so is going to take charge of you. You didn't get hurt and it won't happen again. So forget it."

The girl would wake up at night crying. "Forget it," they would say. Eventually, she did forget it. She pushed it, as any behavioral scientist will tell us, down into her subconscious. But when we push something down, it doesn't disappear. It just goes down, eventually and inevitably to reappear. It could be a matter of years. In her case, it surfaced 30 years later as a recurring nightmare.

I asked the team leader: "How did you know about the planes and the bombs?" She said, "I didn't know. It just came into my head. We had been praying for the guidance of the Lord. When we are open, the Lord simply communicates information to us that we don't have." She had prayed for that and the person was healed. The woman never had the nightmare again. Can we see how God can be present to a person at any stage of his/her life. A very curious and little-known truth.

A famous Canadian brain surgeon by the name of Dr. Wilder Penfield, who lived and worked mainly in Montreal, discovered through research that our subconscious memory holds every single thing that has ever happened to us from the time of conception, although we consciously know only a fraction of what actually is there. Our actual recall is very small compared to our incredible subconscious memory which is like a library of tapes. That's where the different emotional problems reside. My own conclusion is that the Lord is able to take some of the tapes out, simply erase them, and put them back.

If the Lord heals like that, then why does it have to take so long and why does it have to involve a ministry that is so exhausting? I think the answer is that when we persevere together in prayer we learn to love one another more.

What we're talking about here is not faith healing. It is the healing ministry of the Church that Jesus initiated and left with us. People don't get healed by getting pumped up to an emotional state of "Let's do it!" Nor is it to be carried on by saying: "The reason you are not healed is that you don't have enough faith. You were sick, received healing prayer, yet didn't get healed... so it must be your fault. If you had enough faith, you'd be healed." That is bad ministry. And terrible theology. Not everybody is healed. The Lord is able to heal only a certain amount because of the weight of sin, but that as we pray more, as we expect more, he'll heal more.

I don't think the healing ministry of the Church is supposed to be centered on an individual person, although there have been many instances of such down through the ages. A lot of us are familiar with the story of Brother André. Brother André Bessette of Montreal was a very humble Holy Cross brother who prayed a lot for healing. He invoked the assistance of St. Joseph. He became known as the 'miracle worker of Mount Royal'.

In general, though, I believe the healing ministry of the Church is supposed to exist in the body of the faithful. Everybody should be praying for the healing of the sick. If somebody is sick among us, we get the anointing from the priest, but we pray together first. Pray in the family. The more we pray for healing, the more we'll experience it.

The healing ministry of the Church has slipped largely into disuse. Our one task is to recover it. It is the Lord himself who does the work. It is his power. Who knows what he will do in the future? We're in a world swamped with unbelief. We are in a world that needs the power of God. I think the world is going to see it. My own sense, and that means I could very well be wrong, is that the Lord is on the verge of releasing a greater depth of his healing power through the Holy Spirit, particularly as we gather together in the name of Jesus around the Eucharistic table. I have the feeling that the Lord is going to do more and greater healing.

We have seen very few of the greater signs like the healing of ailments such as cerebral palsy, muscular dystrophy, spinal cord injuries, the healing of mental disorders, deep depression, paranoia, schizophrenia, the healing of people born blind, born deaf. Often enough I've been present when someone begins to hear out of an ear that had gone deaf, but I've never seen anybody who was deaf from birth healed in that way. Greater healings are going to happen.

When? The Lord says: "Soon." That's the Lord's timing, by the way. Everything that is going to happen with the Lord is going to happen soon. I can't say I know what that means. With the Lord, a day is as a thousand years. But I think it will be sooner than that.

This is the way I see it, at any rate. We have to recover the Church's healing ministry. We have to be a people who believe in the Lord's Word, who stand on it, who expect it to happen, who pray continually for the healing of those who have needs, whether physical or emotional. That's the kind of people the Lord wants us to be.

Study Questions:

1 Fr. Bob says, "It is God's plan that we enter into wholeness. Woundedness is not his idea... Our problem is sin... That's why Jesus consistently called for repentance. If we want to move towards healing, the first step is always move away from sin."

How does this inspire hope for healing in the wounded areas of your life?

2 Jean Vanier is quoted as saying, "The things that we have been through have shaped us and made us into the people that we are. Our present emotional difficulties stem from past experiences—deprivations, and traumas, mostly."

How have you experienced this in your own life and in the lives of those you love?

3 Fr. Bob reminds us that: "[The] Lord is the one who does the real job of healing. This healing is accomplished through prayer for the healing of memories and is based upon God's omnipresence... If we can get into our past with the Lord's assistance and find out the origin of the problem and invite the Lord into that, he can begin to heal the situation."

Reflecting on the many stories Fr. Bob shares of people encountering inner healing in their lives, we invite you to pray to the Holy Spirit in your own words for any healing that you may need.

CHAPTER NINE

Discipleship

Once he began his short public life, Jesus was joined by a good number of disciples. From these, he chose his twelve Apostles.

What qualified a man to be a disciple of Jesus? If he left all and followed Jesus, he could qualify. If he was willing to forego everything to the Lord—home, spouse, family, property etc—he could be Jesus' disciple. The disciple was one who was sold out for Jesus, sold out for the Kingdom.

Let us love in deed and in truth, and not merely talk about it (1 John 3:18). That means love God, love one another, love our neighbour. We need to be taught, but there comes a time when there is enough of that, and it is time to translate knowing into doing, living the Gospel. Time to get down to business. Jesus preached to the masses: I am the Way, the Truth and the Life. Accept me for who I am. I am the one sent by the Father. Through me the world will have life. Without me you can do nothing. Come to me. That's the first step—coming to terms with Jesus.

Jesus offers salvation. Salvation is life to the full, both now and forever. Death becomes the gateway to eternal life. That's the good news of the Kingdom of God, and Jesus is the one who makes it possible. He preaches to the crowds, he touches and heals the sick in order to catch their attention, and then he gives them the call: Repent. Turn away from what's wrong, turn away from sin, and come to God. Follow me. Come to the Lord. If you will simply do that, salvation will be yours. You will live. This is the Good News.

Not only does Jesus call us to be saved; he calls us to be his disciples as well. Being a disciple of the Lord is more than just being saved. It is entering into friendship with God. Being a disciple is taking on his burden, is getting involved with him in the establishment of the Kingdom of God on earth. Uniting with the Lord, co-operating with him and doing his work—that's what the Lord wants from us. He wants us to be disciples. He wants us to follow him with all of our hearts and souls, and to make everything over to him. If we notice in the Gospel, Jesus talks to different groups. He talks to the crowds, calling them to repent, believe the Good News, and accept him. But again and again, he also takes the disciples aside, and talks to them. He is training them for something special. Disciples were not just members of the crowd, but rather those who had made the decision to follow him completely.

In those days, teachers travelled from town to town sharing their knowledge. They gathered followers. These were loosely called disciples. But being a disciple of Jesus meant something more. Being his disciple meant pulling up roots and following him without reserve. It was the mandate of the Father: Go to the towns of Israel and proclaim the Good News. So he went from one place to another, and those who were going to be his disciples had to leave their dwelling places and go with him. We don't know how long that took. I suspect that most of them left home for a period of time, perhaps a few months to the better part of a year, until they felt they had absorbed enough to carry out his message, and then they went back home. Mary, Martha, and Lazarus in Bethany, for example, were certainly disciples of Jesus, but they lived now at home. I am assuming that they had followed him for a time and now they were back. So, at that time, in order to be disciples, they had to leave everything and follow Jesus for a while, and be taught and coached and prepared. Then they would go back home to form the Church, to be the Church wherever they were. Some of the disciples were called to follow him for life and never return home.

In those days, the people did not have VCRs, tape recorders, or books. But we have all of these today. In order for us to be the same kind of disciples, we don't have to follow Jesus from place to place. We can become disciples of his right where we are, but we do need to decide to make everything available to him, to be taught, and then to be planted as the Church and do his work.

You and I are called to give our whole lives over to the Lord, to follow him with our whole hearts, and be available to him. This teaching—the components of discipleship—is the bottom line, the crunch. I find some of these points rather challenging, and I don't particularly like to be challenged. Possibly others don't like to be challenged either, but, nonetheless, we all need it. We'll have to take the components which challenge us to the Lord in prayer and let him deal with us.

1. Authenticity. If we are going to be disciples of the Lord, we have to be authentic. People will smell us out very quickly if we are phonies. We have to mean what we say. We have to say it and do it. We have to live it out.

There can't be any factions among us. Jesus says: *This is how all will know that you are my disciples, if you have love for one another* (John 13:35 NABRE). We are called to love our neighbours. Everybody in the world is a neighbour to us, but not everybody in the world is a brother or sister. Our brothers and sisters are those who have made the same total commitment to the Lord that we have—presuming we have made it. The Word of God says to love our neighbours as ourselves. The love for the disciples Jesus calls for is a step beyond that. Love one another, he says, as I have loved you. That's how we are to love one another. And how has he loved us? He went to the Cross. He gave away his life. We are called to be people who love one another that way. That's challenging for sure.

"I don't have much in common with her, or with him, or with them." Have we ever said that? That's not quite good enough. The Lord wants us to develop things in common, if necessary, so that we can love one another. We don't have to agree with everybody about everything. We have different styles and ways of responding. But do we really love one another? There can't be any vestige of elitism in our lives. We can't look down our noses at other people. We can't be saying: "I have greater gifts than they have." The gifts that the Lord gives are not related to education. They are not related to economic situation. They are not related to anything. Jesus says: *Not everyone who says to me 'Lord, Lord' will enter the kingdom of heaven, but only* [*those*] *who do the will of my Father in heaven* (Matt 7:21 NABRE).

The bottom line of authenticity is doing the Father's will. It's not enough to look good, or holy, or pious. Doing the Father's will—that's being authentic. Jesus says: *If you love me, keep my commandments* (John 14:21 paraphrase).

2. Priorities. If I become a disciple of Jesus, my priorities will have to change. This means taking on the Lord's own burden. Jesus says: *Come to me all you who labour and are overburdened, and I will give you rest,* [*for*] *my yoke is easy, and my burden light* (Matt 11:28,30 JB). In other words, he is saying to give him our burdens and he will give us his. It's light. His burden is the conversion of the whole world. Although that doesn't sound too light, he promises us the power of the Holy Spirit.

We don't have to be clever or highly gifted. We just have to be available. One of the things I say everyday when I pray is "Lord, if you want to use me, use me. Show me what you want me to do. Whatever it is, I'll do it. I have very few gifts. I'm not ready, but I'm available. I'm willing." Our priorities have to become the Lord's own priorities. We have to be able to identify with the heart of God and to share in his pain. I assume that God Almighty, our loving Father, looking upon this battered and bruised world, is extremely pained to see it. That's the kind of heart that we need to take on. We have to share his pain and his desire to see his love take over in the world. We have to identify with him. Jesus says: *Seek first the Kingdom of God, and all other things will be added to you* (Matt 6:33 ESV). That's the disciple's watch word. Seek first the Kingdom of God.

Unless the Lord build the house, they labour in vain who [*try*] (Ps 127:1). It is God's power, his grace, that will make it go. We don't have it. The disciple places him or herself fully at the disposal of the Lord. We can relate to what St. Paul says: *I have reappraised* [*everything*] *as loss in the light of the surpassing knowledge of my Lord, Jesus Christ. For his sake, I have forfeited everything. I have come to count all else as rubbish so that he may be my wealth* (Phil 3:7-8). That's a disciple talking. He goes on: *I have not yet reached it, I have not finished the course, but I am racing to capture the prize for which Christ Jesus captured me* (Phil 3:12 paraphrase). That's a good description of a disciple—one whom Jesus has captured. We are captives of the Lord. He has captured our hearts and he wants to harness us and put us to work for him.

Taking on the Lord's priorities—that is what a disciple will do.

3. Grace. The disciple will treasure and cling desperately to the state of grace. St. Paul writes: *Do not receive the grace of God in vain* (2 Cor 6:1). The grace of God is friendship with the Lord. The author of Hebrews writes: *See to it that no* [*one*] *falls away from the grace of God* (Heb 12:15). We are to live in the state of grace. St. Paul again: *We have gained access by faith to the* [*state of*] *grace in which we now stand* (Rom 5:2). Peter writes in his second letter: *Grow in the grace and the knowledge of our*

Lord and Saviour, Jesus Christ (2 Pet 3:18). We have to hang on to that incredible gift of God—intimacy with him. Living fully for the Lord now, and then living forever with him, is the goal of human life. If we gain the whole world and miss that, we have nothing.

The disciple will treasure the state of grace—friendship with God.

4. ***Holiness.*** The disciple will strive for holiness. Righteousness is great. Goodness and the state of grace are fantastic. But they are not good enough. It is not only good people that the Lord is after. It is holy people. Holiness is not just something for the great heroes and heroines of God, not just for the canonized saints, or for the clergy. The holiness of God is meant for us all. We have to be perfectly purified of all the barnacles and obstacles to the life of grace in order that we might be able to live with God. *You shall be holy because I am holy,* says the Lord (Lv 11:45). Jesus put it this way: *You must be perfect, just as your heavenly Father is perfect* (Matt 5:48). That doesn't mean we are supposed to be God, but we do have to be perfect in our own state as human beings. Otherwise, we won't fit in.

We have to be purified and made perfect, and we might as well allow the Lord to begin this work on us now. That's moving towards holiness—entering into the fullness of God's plan for us.

I remember being at a meeting of diocesan youth groups a few years ago. We were talking about the problem of youth ministry in the Church. We were asking what was happening with our young people. And what really works. There were representatives from different groups from around town. There might have been a dozen or fifteen groups represented, and each one was invited at some point to talk about his or her particular perspectives on the matter. We heard different reports about what they thought was working: this program and that program, this social and that dance. But nobody was talking about a relationship with the Lord. It was as though he was not part of the agenda, but was on the outside looking in.

When it came my turn, I said my usual thing: "I think the first object of our youth work should be introducing our young people to a relationship with their Saviour. Our religion is not so much following a set of rules, not so much membership in an organization, although those things are important. Our faith is basically a relationship with the person of Jesus. The number one priority in our youth ministry should be bringing our young people to an encounter with the risen Christ himself."

That didn't go over too well. I got a lot of rather odd looks. One young lady was brave enough to respond, "I can't relate to that. I'm young. I have a lot of living to do. I'm not ready to be a saint yet. I want to have some fun first, before I get that serious." I found myself saying, "You mean to say that you don't really know that it's the saints that have the most fun?" She gave me the strangest look, as if to say, "Are you ever out of it!" I began to think, "Well, maybe I am." I certainly did not fit in that night.

The Lord is after holiness, that total all-out commitment to follow him with everything we are and everything we do.

5. The daily cross. *If you want to be a disciple of mine, Jesus says, then you must take up your cross every day and follow along after me* (Luke 9:23 paraphrase). He describes it further: *You see this little grain of wheat? Unless it fall into the earth and die, all it will ever be is just a little germ of wheat. But, if it does so fall and die, it will produce tremendous, abundant results—a harvest* (John 12:24 paraphrase). Fantastic! He was offering that to us as an example of what we need to do. We have to get rid of those things that drag us down. That's dying continually. And he called it the daily cross.

We don't have to search out the cross. It will find us. The question is: what do we do with it when it comes? We embrace it. What is it like? Being misunderstood can be a considerable cross. Bad motives attributed to me is not fair. Simply accepting it, embracing the daily cross—that's what Jesus asks us to do.

St. Teresa of Avila experienced a fair bit of the daily cross in her life. She put it this way: "Lord, if this is how you treat your friends, it's no wonder you don't have very many." In the best spirit of the Psalms, she was doing a little holy complaining. I recommend it. I find I get my best results in prayer, in fact, when I complain to the Lord.

Jesus says: *If you lose your life, you will save it* (Mark 8:35 GNB). Since the Gospel contradicts the world, if we are living it, we're going to draw some flack. We may not really want it, but it's going to happen, nonetheless. It will follow us around. But Jesus says not to worry about it: *Blessed are you if you are persecuted for my sake, if you are insulted or slandered. Rejoice and be glad, because your reward in heaven will be great* (Matt 5:11-12 paraphrase). And, strangely enough, the Prince of Peace brings, not peace but discord and turmoil. *You think I have come to bring peace? I haven't. I have come to bring the sword. I've come to bring division. There will be mother set against daughter and father against son.* (Luke 12:51-52 paraphrase). Division is not what the Lord wants, but it will happen just the same.

Do we want to know what the cross is? And the sword? Again and again, I have seen it happen that one spouse wants to make a total commitment to the Lord, while the other doesn't want to have anything to do with it. There's the division. The relationship weakens. That's the cross. It's the same thing with a son or a daughter who comes into a whole new relationship with the Lord and life begins to change. If the parents are not ready for it, there is division.

I can remember getting phone calls when I was teaching. Some of the students were entering into a whole new relationship with the Lord. They were hungering for his Word. They were reading the Bible in their rooms at home at night. And in some cases, unfortunately, it posed a tremendous threat to the parents. A typical telephone call would go: "What's going on with my son? He's reading the Bible in his bedroom every night. He's only 16 years old. What are you people doing to him over there?" That's division. That's the daily cross. So what do we do with it? Pick it up, Jesus says, and carry it along after me.

It is no coincidence, I guess, that the whole concept is neatly encapsulated in the very name of our community—The Companions of the Cross. We have had a few slings and arrows. I have been called a 'cult master'. I don't particularly like to hear things like that. I don't think it's fair, but what am I supposed to do? The Lord says to pick up the cross and carry it. To rejoice in it, in fact, he adds. I have had trouble rejoicing over it, but I really find that, as I do, the Lord works through it.

Blessed are you, Jesus says, if you are persecuted for my sake. Don't worry about it. I'm taking care of you. Embrace the cross.

6. Prayer. A person who wants to be a disciple of Jesus is going to commit a regular time every day to prayer. I have to spend time with the Lord and discuss everything with him, listen to him, consult him, give him honour and praise, read his Word.

A time of prayer every day for the disciple is without question.

7. Fasting. The disciple is going to fast. The Pharisees came to Jesus one day and asked him a question: *Rabbi, why is it that the disciples of John the Baptist and we Pharisees fast and your disciples do not?* Jesus' answer explains to us what fasting is all about: *There is no point in the friends of the bridegroom fasting when the bridegroom is still with them, but when the bridegroom is gone, then they will fast* (*cf.* Luke 5:33-35; Matt 9:14-15). As we pull away from things we depend upon in the material, fleshly sense, we are able to be more spiritually alive and open to the Lord. That's the way it works.

Do we fast? It's supposed to be part of our response as disciples.

Jesus took it for granted we would because he told us that when we fast, we should not look glum like these Pharisees. They look as though they are carrying the weight of the world. Don't look like them, he urges. Turn on a smile when you fast. He did not say 'if you fast'; he said, 'when you fast'. Fasting can be a powerful dynamic.

I hesitate even to mention it, but fasting can be overdone. The fast we heard recommended from Medjugorje was bread and water for 24 hours. That's a good way to fast if we can do it. But some people can't handle that, though. They say the bread sits in the stomach like a lump of dough, and they find it difficult to concentrate. Others say they get crashing headaches when they try to withdraw from caffeine for 24 hours. One nun, who is probably one of the most dignified women I have ever met, tried to do that anyway, and she lost all her strength. She literally could not stand up. Friday was a wipeout. She had to stay in her room. She described how she had to get to the bathroom on her hands and knees. In her own situation, it was simply too much.

Some people who have tried fasting and have not been able to handle it, quit altogether—not what the Lord would want, I don't think. If we can't handle the bread and water fast, we can do something less. But we need to do something. We can give up one meal, or part of a meal, or dessert, or take lesser portions. I'm afraid I'm one of the people who can't tamper with my food program. There are other ways to fast. How about the newspaper—not reading it one day a week? Or not at all for that matter? Television?—it wouldn't hurt to cut down or out that. And the radio, too, for that matter. We can pick up the Bible instead, and read a few verses. How does that sound? It's possible. And, take it from me, it's very freeing.

In some way, the disciple of the Lord will respond to the Lord's call to some kind of fast on a regular basis.

8. Confession. The wisdom of the Lord says: *Confess your sins* *to one another* (Jas 5:16 JB). Over the centuries, we have been able to do it with a representative of the Church, one specially designated and ordained for the purpose. In it, we celebrate the Lord's forgiveness.

The condition for forgiveness is repentance. It is turning away from sin: Lord, I'm sorry; I don't want to do that again. I want to stay away from that. Forgiven! Since this sacrament is the celebration of that forgiveness, it is filled with the Lord's presence. If we approach it in faith, God will work through it.

Though sins be forgiven, we still need, in serious cases, to be reconciled with the Church, the whole body. The official representative, the ordained priest, can accomplish that.

I have seen Confession work tremendously in people's lives. I find what happens very often is that people in the Sacrament of Confession are set free from one thing or other. Even when we are forgiven, unconfessed sin seems to retain some kind of power to control us. The Sacrament of Penance is able to take care of a lot of that, if we enter into it with expectancy. In this sacrament, we can also experience the healing of the roots of sin and so stay free more easily.

9. The Sabbath. We have to keep holy the Sabbath Day. The earliest Christians were Jewish who wanted to remain faithful to the synagogue on Saturday, their Sabbath Day. So they celebrated the Breaking of the Bread in their homes on Sunday, the first day of the week. The Church changed it to Sunday, the day of Jesus' resurrection, using the authority Jesus had given it.

So how do we spend the Sabbath? What are we doing with it now? Obviously, we need to gather together to worship the Lord. But what about the rest of the day? Is Sunday any different from other days for us? It should be. There should be some kind of family component, or some kind of quiet time. It doesn't mean we can't do anything else. Jesus did not hesitate to minister on the Sabbath. But Sunday needs to have a different tone to it, a different pace. That's keeping holy the Sabbath Day. I think it's important for us to review this. It's quite possible that we might be out of order in the Lord's eyes for the way we keep, or do not keep, the Sabbath Day. The disciple needs to have a good look at just how he/she does in that regard.

10. Hospitality. St. Paul writes: *Make hospitality your special care* (Rom 12:13 JB). We have to make room in our lives for other people. I have to be ready to sacrifice some of my own comfort, some of my own time, for other people. Every day the Lord will lead people unexpectedly across my path. What do I do then? How do I respond to it? Do I have time for people?

I personally try to follow a schedule. I draw up my daily program. It is important. Unfortunately, it can become too important. To a certain degree, of course, I have to have an agenda, but my feathers get ruffled when my schedule is disturbed. I think this type of thing speaks to me about the question of hospitality. I'm afraid I fall short here. I don't have enough time for people. I don't have enough time for small things, or things that seem small to me. I continually fight to try to be more available to people. That's what hospitality is.

Hospitality has to do, not so much with accepting people into our homes, as it is accepting people into our lives on a regular basis.

The author of Hebrews says: *Don't neglect hospitality. In this way some have entertained angels without knowing it* (Heb 13:2). These may be literal angels at times or simply people that are sent by God.

The question of hospitality is one that very personally challenges me. Are there some readers who can relate to that?

11. Privacy. This is related to hospitality. If I am going to be hospitable, I have to be ready to give up some of my privacy, and maybe a lot of it. Do I like my privacy? I think we all like a certain amount of it, and probably a certain amount of privacy is a human necessity, but maybe not as much as we think.

I remember visiting a young man whom I had taught in high school. He was living full time as one of about twenty applicants at Madonna House in Combermere, with about 150 other people. They have a certain training program to undergo.

He lived in a little cabin that must have been about 15' by 15', with a privy outside. Five applicants shared the cabin. The bunks were all lined up against one wall, with about 12 inches separating each. There was one dresser, and it had five drawers in it—one each. There was a hanging rack for coats and whatever else, and they each had a little section there. And there was a little stove that kept the place more or less warm. I looked at it and was lost for words.

A year later I was in the same cabin, and this time there were nine in it. In order to accommodate the other four, they had slung bunks from the ceiling, and added another chest of four drawers. I said to my friend: You don't have any privacy. He looked at me with a kind of smile and said: 'I have practically no privacy, but, after all, privacy is a luxury.' I was profoundly challenged.

The drive back from Combermere which follows the route through the hills, takes me two hours and five minutes. I wrestled with his concept of privacy for about an hour and a half of that time, continually talking it back and forth with the Lord, actually arguing with him. By the time I was back into town, I was saying to myself: you know, he's probably right. The privacy that we have and insist on in our dwellings and in our whole lives is probably more than we need. Most people in our world have nothing like it.

Are we willing to give some of our privacy? A good question. What is the Lord saying to us about it?

12. Simplicity. The world is clearly divided into the haves and the have-nots. We will have to take a prophetic stand if we are going to be disciples of the Lord. It looks as though Jesus lived a rather simple lifestyle. *The Son of Man has nowhere to lay his head* (Matt 8:20). We are supposed to be challenged by that and question the style of life that we live. How simple is it? I think my own lifestyle is simple enough, but I am consulting the Lord about what it should be. Should it be simpler? I think a lot of it has to do with sharing things and sharing space.

13. Stewardship. The disciple has to settle the question of ownership. Who owns my house, my apartment, my furniture, my car, my stereo set, my summer cottage, my bank account, and whatever else I have? The world tells us that we ourselves own the things we have. What the Lord is saying is just the opposite. He owns it all. We are simply stewards or managers of the things that the Lord has given us. We are not the owners.

How do I settle the ownership question? I have to say, "Lord, whatever I have is yours. If you want to call for part of it, or all of it, it's yours." No more can I say, "What's mine is mine." Rather, what's mine belongs to God.

14. Tithing. Have we all seen that rather clever cartoon? Four people are gathered in a small cluster outside church on Sunday morning—the pastor with a wife and husband, the wife carrying a very small child.

Both the child and the man are crying profusely. The pastor asks the mother, "What's bothering your baby?" The mother responds, "He's teething." "And what about your husband?" the pastor queries. "He's tithing," she says.

The Lord's word to the Jewish people was very specific. Everyone was required to give ten percent, a tithe, of certain agricultural products that they produced. There are over 30 references in the Old Testament to tithing.

Jesus encouraged even more giving. The early Christians opted for a very radical response to that. In Acts 2:42, we are told that they went into a total sharing situation, something akin to the Communist ideal, where everybody gives in everything he earns, and receives back what he needs. That did not endure as a common practice in the Church, but it did give the signal for later developments in religious communities as the centuries rolled on.

Pope Leo XIII taught that the amount that we are obliged to give varies with ones economic circumstances:

> "No one is commanded to distribute to others that which is required for his own necessities and those of his household; nor even to give away what is reasonably required to keep up becomingly his condition in life; 'for no one ought to live unbecomingly'. But when necessity has been supplied, and one's position fairly considered, it is a duty to give to the indigent out of that which is over."[6]

I am convinced the Lord is calling for a serious review of tithing today—one-tenth of my total earnings. The reactions of some? "Not gross earnings," they'll say, "surely it's net." Actually it is gross. It sounds like a tough call. But we really have to try it before we can reject the idea. It is really not as painful as we think. In fact, it is usually incredibly blessed.

I did not always tithe, but I do now and have for several years. In fact, I make it around 40%. When I was first ordained, I was appointed to a rather large parish in the east end of the city. There was a pastor there and another priest who was also an assistant, but a few years older than I. The assistant was quite literally the most generous person I have ever met. He gave away almost everything. He was continually handing out money—pull-

6 Pope Leo XIII, *Rerum novarum*, referencing St. Thomas Aquinas, *Summa Theologica*, IIa, IIae, 32, a6.

ing it out of his pocket and handing it to this one and that. He even gave his clothes away—shoes, socks, jackets etc.

It led him into some amusing situations. A chap came to the door one day when it was raining. He had a bad pair of shoes on, and his feet were all wet. This priest took the shoes off his own feet, and gave them to him. He forgot, however, that he was doing a wedding the next day, and that he had only one pair of shoes, except for a pair of running shoes which he did not feel were proper for the wedding. The next morning, when he looked under the bed for his shoes, he remembered that he had given them away. I was out that day. He rummaged through my closet with no luck since I too had only one pair of shoes. He had very small feet—size 7, I think, which is fairly small for a man. The pastor, who had several pairs of shoes, and was also away, wore size 13. What the younger priest had to do was to take a pair of the pastor's shoes, stuff newspapers in the toes, put elastics around the shoes, put on an alb that was about five inches too long, and flop around during the wedding. Later, he gave me a hard time for having only one pair of shoes! I said: "But you only had one pair of shoes and now you have none." "That's different," he said.

He very absolutely gave everything away. He even gave his car away one day! A family in the parish had a car which was run down. One day it just died. So he gave them his car. I said, "What are you going to do? How are you going to get around?" He said, "I'll take the bus. I'll get a bicycle." I thought, "Wow! Very radical!" Two weeks later somebody came in from nowhere, and gave him another car, a better one than he'd given away.

This fellow was like a depot, with things coming in and going out all the time. His needs were always taken care of. He didn't run short of anything. He was fine. I saw tithing work in him. He was blessed in so many ways. He had a very happy disposition. People were always giving him things. One day a parishioner came to the door to say goodbye. He was leaving the parish. He asked for this generous assistant by name. I said: "I'm sorry, but he's away today." He said: "Well, perhaps you could give him this envelope. It has $75 in it." Now, $75 back 30 years ago was a lot of money. It is still a nice sum today, but then it was a lot more. He gave him $75. I didn't get a nickel. That's the way it was working.

I saw tithing work, but I didn't pick it up right away. It took me several years to get smart enough, or obedient enough, to do it. Up until that time, I was always budgeting carefully, scrimping, balancing columns, and just making it. When I started to tithe, my monetary difficulties disappeared. I can't explain it, but with tithing everybody gets blessed. It blesses the work to which we give our resources, and it blesses us in a very real way.

I can only see it, I think, in the light of the Lord's own word, spoken through the prophet Malachi. *Bring the whole tithe into the storehouse ... and try me in this, says the Lord of Hosts: Shall I not open for you the floodgates of heaven, to pour down blessing upon you without measure?* (Mal 3:10). In other words, if we are generous with God, he has guaranteed he will take care of us.

Where should the tithe go? Most of it should go to the place where one receives spiritual food. The ordinary recipient of most of the tithes will be the parish attended. And all parishes have many needs, well beyond the simple keeping of the doors open.

For example, a while back, I met two different people who were in absolute shambles. One big strong fellow was the father of a family with a wife and three children. He came to me with tears streaming down his face. I said: "What's the matter? Are you OK?" "Oh, I don't know," he said, "but something is happening inside me today." The Lord was touching him. I have seen this so often that I don't question it anymore.

That same Sunday there was a young woman, about 30 or so, crying and sobbing. I asked her the same thing: "Are you

OK?" "Something happened to me in church today," she said. I replied: "I think the Lord is just trying to get your attention." "He's got it," she said. "He's got my attention."

People like these need to be followed up. Somebody with intelligence, sensitivity, perhaps a bit of training, plus the Lord's call for it, needs to be recruited (and paid, I would think).

In addition, people who begin to grow in their relationship with the Lord and in their faith need someone to guide them along. This all-important work might require yet another full-time person.

Where do we stand on it? What do we teach? We promote tithing. The full disciple will take it on, and will very literally give 10% of his or her gross earnings to the work of the Lord.

15. Almsgiving. Over and above the 10% tithe, the Scriptures speak of giving alms. *Prayer and fasting are good, but better than either is almsgiving* (Tob 12:8). Jesus himself said: *When you give alms, your left hand must not know what your right hand is doing* (Matt 6:3 JB). He didn't say: 'If'. He said: 'When'.

But we are to give according to our means, not beyond. The relief of others is not intended to impoverish us. There is need for a certain balance. St. Paul says: *Your plenty at the present time should supply their need, so that their surplus may one day* [*meet*] *your need* (2 Cor 8:14). In other words, we are all one body together and we give what we can. We're even supposed to smile while we're doing it. Paul says again: *Everyone must give according to what he has inwardly decided, not sadly or grudgingly. For God loves a cheerful giver* (2 Cor 9:7).

16. Work. I used to tell the students at school that work was probably the dirtiest four-letter word in the English language. They knew what I meant. It is not something to do as little of as possible, or to try to avoid. The Lord's Word says it: *Six days you are to work. The seventh is the Lord's Sabbath* (Exod 20:9-10 paraphrase). We usually emphasize the seventh—the Sabbath.

But the other part of it has to do with working the other six days. We have never thought of it as a command of the Lord, most people would say. Nonetheless, it is. We are supposed to work in whatever way we can—not drive ourselves to exhaustion doing more work than we're able. But we are expected to work.

St. Paul clears up any uncertainty for us and tells us how important it is: *Let him who will not work, not eat* (2 Thes 3:10). That seems rather direct. Writing to Titus he says: *Be ready to take any honest employment* (Titus 3:1).

But we should avoid being super-spiritual. I remember talking to a student of mine whose academic situation was in a total shambles. I taught school for 20 years and have seen thousands of reports. His report was the worst report I've ever seen in my life. However, this young chap was very serious about the Lord, very prayerful. At the behest of his mother, I had a little session with him. "You are serious about the Lord," I said. "Do you realize that your work as a student is a religious obligation?" "No," he said, "what do you mean?" "Your call from God," I said, "is to be a student. If you aren't putting a lot into it, and at least getting by in school, you are offending the law of God." That was the beginning of quite another conversion for him, as his mother can attest.

17. Time. We have to budget our time. The disciple is expected to have a look at where he or she is spending it. How much of it do we give to our families? How much do we give to work? How much to the Lord? We should consult him about all that. There needs to be a good balance, neither too lax nor too scrupulous.

18. Conversation. The Lord calls those who would be disciples of Jesus to put their tongues in order. Even those who are dedicated to the Lord and trying to follow him can very quickly offend with the tongue. We can do untold damage with our mouths.

All of us fall short in many respects. If a person is without fault in speech he is a man in the fullest sense, because he can control his entire body. When we put bits in the mouths of horses to make them obey us, we guide the rest of their bodies. It is the same with ships. However large they are, and despite the fact that they are driven by fierce winds, they are directed by very small rudders on whatever course the steersman's impulse may select. The tongue is something like that. It is a small member; yet it makes great pretensions. See how tiny the spark is that sets a huge forest ablaze. The tongue is such a flame. It exists among our members as a whole universe of malice. The tongue defiles the entire body. Its flames encircle our course from birth, and its fire is kindled by hell. Every form of life—four-footed or winged, crawling or swimming—can be tamed, and has been tamed by mankind. The tongue, no man can tame. It is a restless evil, full of deadly poison. We use it to say; 'Praised be the Lord and Father.' Then we use it to curse men though they are made in the likeness of God. Blessing and curse come out of the same mouth. This ought not to be, my brothers (Jas 3:2-10)!

James, as usual, pulls no punches.

Each of us must review our manner of speech. How much do I talk? What do I talk about? How much do I talk about myself? How much of my conversation deals with me? How much of it deals with other people in critical terms?

19. Relaxation. This is important. We can both overdo and underdo relaxation, and either way we will stall our growth. We have to find healthy and constructive ways to relax, while guarding the entrance to our minds. What kind of use do I make of television, magazines, soap operas, videos, movies—all of which can be subtly bending our attitudes? Or am I content to bury myself in my work and thus probably retreat from important issues I should be addressing?

20. The body, the temple of the Holy Spirit. If we will take care of our bodies, they will serve us well and enable us to serve God better. Some years ago the Lord convicted me of this. I was teaching at a school where the students' council decided upon a little scheme to raise some money for a project.

They organized a contest and charged $2.00 an entry. The object was to guess the total weight of the staff. For two weeks all the students went around looking us over. When the time came for the decision, every staff member had to weigh in at a school assembly. I tipped the scales at close to 220 pounds. I couldn't believe it! They had been calling me Big Bob. Now I knew why.

At that point, I decided that some things had to change. I began to exercise seriously and watch what I ate. That was about thirty years ago. It worked. In a few months, I had my weight down to 180 and felt a great deal better. Instead of having to stop at the top of each set of stairs, I could now go three flights, two steps at a time and not breathe heavily at all. I don't think I could have done the things that I've done the last few years, kept up the pace I've felt called to maintain, if I hadn't done something about my health. I believe that was a definite call from the Lord. I can see his hand in it.

It is something we tend to dismiss. We can easily become super-spiritual. "We don't need to get on a health kick," we'll say. "The really important things are prayer and ministry and gifts of the Lord. Our bodies are not important. We don't have to worry about them." But that's not being truly human. We are supposed to be fully alive as human beings, but we can't be if we let our bodies go. Not to worry. It's never too late to start correcting the situation.

I wonder how people like Abraham and Moses and some of the others in the Bible were able to carry on so effectively for so long? Could it have been because they did not do violence to their bodies the way we do? They lived a vigorous lifestyle and had a simpler food program.

The main sins here are gluttony and sloth, things we tend to ignore. We're not gluttonous most of the day except when we sit at table. Nutrition combats gluttony. Overeating, and eating the wrong kind of food, is a national epidemic. It's important for us to learn the principles of nutrition. It's important to have a rule of life.

Wine has been the ruin of many (Sir 31:25). We know the devastation that alcohol has worked in so many people's lives. Do we need it? We take into our bodies things that are not doing us much good. I myself have a weakness for sugar. I love the taste, but 20 minutes afterwards, I'm semi-depressed. When I give up sugar for an extended time, I feel much better. I should look upon it as a poison and stay away from it altogether. *Moderate eating ensures sound slumber and a clear mind upon rising. Distress, anguish, loss of sleep, restless tossing—these are the lot of the glutton* (Sir 31:20).

Exercise can serve to combat sloth. There is *no treasure greater than a healthy body* (Sir 30:16). The Lord can use the healthy body much better than one that isn't. St. Paul writes: *I discipline my body* [*in order to*] *master it* (1 Cor 9:27). If we don't master the body, it will master us. There's far too much pampering of the body. How much do I give in to it? Getting up in the morning is a key. This isn't a gift. It's a decision that will become a skill if I stay with it.

These, as I see it, are the main components in the life of the disciple.

Salvation is a gift. All it costs is the decision to follow the Lord and turn away from sin, which will only hurt us and destroy us anyway. So, in a sense, it doesn't cost anything. Salvation is free.

Discipleship is another matter. There is a cost here. Jesus talks about the fellow who goes to build a tower: *Now, what kind of man is going to go ahead and start to build a tower without first making sure he has all the materials? If he doesn't don't do that, everyone is going to laugh at him* (Luke 14:28-29 paraphrase). He goes on to make reference to the king who is considering going to war against another king who has two or three times the number of soldiers available. If he goes ahead, Jesus is saying, he is not very wise. The king has got to be prepared. In other words, he's telling the disciples that he surely wants them and even needs them. In fact he's asking for something quite radical. He wants their whole lives. But he doesn't want them to make such a far-reaching decision without first counting the cost. *My son, when you come to serve the Lord, prepare yourself for trials* (Sir 2:1). It will cost us everything to be disciples of the Lord, but that's what he wants from us. And, of course, the rewards are everlasting.

Study Questions:

1 Fr. Bob lists twenty components in life that are integral to a disciple of Jesus. Which of these components challenge you the most and why? Fr. Bob instructs us to "take the components which challenge us to the Lord in prayer and let him deal with us."

2 Commenting on Luke 14:28-29, Fr. Bob says Jesus is asking his disciples "for something quite radical. He wants their whole lives. But he doesn't want them to make such a far-reaching decision without first counting the cost... It will cost us everything to be disciples of the Lord, but that's what he wants from us. And, of course, the rewards are everlasting."

Are you truly prepared to give up everything to be a disciple of Jesus and receive his everlasting rewards?

3 Fr. Bob exhorts us to be available to God. In order to help you become more fully available to the Lord, we encourage you to pray the following discipleship prayer of Fr. Bob's:

Lord, if you want to use me, use me. Show me what you want me to do. Whatever it is, I'll do it. I have very few gifts. I'm not ready, but I'm available. I'm willing.

CHAPTER TEN

The Condition of The Church and the World

We live in a fairly messed-up world, and it might just be getting messier. I don't want to sound negative, but we need to understand the situation we live in, to look at it and say: "That's the way things are," and "This is what we have to do about it." There's no point in bemoaning it all or saying: "Isn't it awful? What a disaster!" The point of this chapter is not simply to lament or to cast aspersions, but rather to understand why we are where we are, and to give some notion of where we can go. To be more exact, we have to hear what God has to say about it.

These are perilous times. Communism has broken down in Eastern Europe, leaving in its wake major economic collapse and opening the door to moral decay, a specialty of the western democratic nations. The nuclear arms race may be slowing down a bit, but it continues nonetheless. We have multiple kill potential on all sides. We have 10 or 12 nations now in what's euphemistically called the 'Nuclear Club'.

The world is split economically, between the nations of the First

World and those of the Third. This imbalance is based, to a large degree, on a history of exploitation of the poorer countries by the richer. We are on the favourable end of the scale because we live in the 'have' world, but the 'have not' section is vast and the imbalance and the contrast are striking. We have runaway inflation in a lot of the developing nations. National debts are rising. Levels of unemployment are maintained because we are told they are necessary. This robs millions of their basic human dignity. It is important for us to be able to work and to earn our way, if we can. That's the Lord's plan for us. The third commandment says: *Six days shall you labour. The seventh is a day of rest* (Exod 23:12 paraphrase).

Each night, all over the world, people go to bed hungry. Yet our potential here in Canada for producing food has barely been tapped. We could be producing far more food here than we do and feeding a much larger segment of the world than we are. At times our governments even pay farmers not to produce, and yet there are people starving. This is certainly not in line with God's plan.

We have assaulted the environment. We have wrested resources from the earth. We have polluted the atmosphere.

So many of our people are victims of chemical abuse. Crack cocaine is tearing the hearts out of some of our cities and is soaring to epidemic proportions.

People are being abused. Young and old are subject to it. Women and children are particularly vulnerable to physical, emotional, and sexual abuse.

There is a crisis in masculinity across the land. To a great extent, men have abdicated their roles and their responsibilities. Men have opted out, and left the managing of home and family to women. Women have taken up the task as best they can, but they can rarely substitute for men with success. Generations of unaffirmed men are becoming either spineless, afraid to take a stand on things, or overly aggressive to mask their insecurities.

There's a crisis in public morality as well. The entertainment industry is doing things today that would not have been tolerated a generation ago. I was recently talking to a woman who had turned on the television one afternoon around 4 p.m. (prime time for children) to check out what the youngsters were being exposed to. "It was horrible," she said. "From one channel to the next it was sex, violence, guns and murder."

It is standard, it would seem, for governments continually to be embarrassed by members who are involved in one type of scandal or other. When a prominent member of the Canadian Parliament was quizzed about an irregular relationship—at the time, he was living with a woman to whom he was not married—he said, "Well, after all, this is the twentieth century, you know, not the Victorian age." He's right. Pre-marital sex is almost taken for granted. Condoms are for sale in a number of our high schools. The cure for AIDS is something called 'safe sex'. Marriage statistics are discouraging.

There's an assault on the unborn. It's incredible when we think of it. Mothers are actually hiring professionals to kill their unborn children.

There is a rise in violence and the suicide rate, especially among the young.

How do we like all that? It could easily demoralize us. It is not pessimism, however. I'm optimistic. I think the Lord is on the move. I think God is going to turn the whole thing around, and I'm just cheering him on: "Go for it, Lord! Get in there! Change things! Purify! Do whatever you have to do!" Every morning I root on the Holy Spirit: "Go for it, Holy Spirit! You are welcome here—in my life and in the life of God's people. You are welcome to do what the Father wants done. Bring forth the Kingdom of God." If we can commit ourselves to doing the will of God, our Father, then things can begin to come into line.

We can only begin to move towards a solution to a problem if we first recognize the problem itself. Otherwise we will be paralyzed. I'm filled with hope, but I believe we have to look at things in a realistic way.

Some people ask the question: "How can God be good, yet create such an incredible shambles?" The answer? He didn't create the mess. We did. God created things to work, to function properly in peace and in justice. That's God's world. The rest of it is our doing. We have contrived this. We have done it ourselves. "But how could a loving God allow it?" others would ask. He has to. If the Lord has made us free, then he has to honour what he has done. He can't take away our freedom. We say God is all-powerful. In one sense he is; yet in another sense he isn't because he can't take away our freedom. He can't contradict what he's already established because, if we weren't free, we could not respond to the Good News. We could not live with him and share his life. We have to be like him in order to be part of his life. We have to be free, and because we are free, we can choose other than his way. Pope John Paul II says that our free will is a great gift, but that it's a tremendous problem as well.

The human race is in a basic state of rebellion against God. Any of us who have sinned (and we all have) are part of the problem. Our sins have piled up and now weigh heavily upon human society, so heavily that it has cracked and buckled in many ways. We can't save ourselves. We need to be saved. We need the Saviour who was sent by the Father.

A few years ago, somebody said to me that the weight of sin now is the heaviest that it's ever been in the history of mankind. When I first heard it, I had difficulty with the notion because I had taught ancient and medieval history in high school and I knew that some of the societies of the past were very evil. Things have been worse, I thought, and in a sense they have. Public morality, for example, has been at a lower ebb at other times in history. How could the weight of sin be so heavy now?

I puzzled about it until someone else explained that the current population of the world is equal to the total population of all previous generations. It then became understandable to me as to why the weight of sin is so heavy now. There are more of us to rebel against God.

Some people say things go in cycles. Right now, they feel, although we are on the way down, we'll soon be on the way up again. We'll recover. Maybe so, but I think that's being a little unrealistic. Things don't have to bounce back. It's quite possible they can just continue to get worse. God wants to show us how to get things turned around. But we'll have to learn how to rely on him.

It is my personal opinion—this is from me and not from the Lord (*cf.* 1 Cor 7:25), as St. Paul wrote in one of his letters—that as we rebel against God, nature will rebel against us. The incidence of natural disasters probably increases in proportion to the increase in human sin.

A question: Have we sinned strictly on our own, or have we had some help? St. Paul has the answer: *Our battle is not against* [*flesh and blood*] *but against the principalities and the powers, the rulers of this world of darkness, the evil spirits in the regions above* (Eph 6:12). The real fight, then, is against the evil spirits who roam throughout the world seeking whom they might devour (*cf.* 1 Pet 5:8), as St. Peter has said in one of his letters.

The world today, including a lot of people within the Church, regards Satan as a kind of myth, a way to describe evil happenings. And yet, Jesus in the Gospels went about expelling demons and saw them flee screaming. A lot of people, including many scholars, maintain it is just a way of speaking, a psychological insight, that gives us a better understanding of these phenomena. But the Church still stands with its original statement concerning evil: there is a person called the devil with evil spirits at his beck and call, and these can interfere with us if we let them. To the degree that we are sinful, we open the door for the action of Satan's minions.

In 1975, Pope Paul VI issued a statement on the devil, whom he called an ugly reality, a malevolent personal being. The official teaching of the Church is very clear and has never changed. It says that there is such a spirit as the spirit of evil, the ancient enemy called Satan, and this is our main fight. It's important for us to understand that and not brush it under the rug saying: "I'd rather not deal with the matter." I'd rather not deal with it either, but I would be foolish if I didn't. The spiritual realm is very real. The Lord God created angels; and the truth is that some of them have rebelled against him. We ignore this fact at our peril. The battle rages around us and we ourselves are the prize. Our minds are the main object of this largely unseen battle. However, unseen though it be, its effects are quite evident.

Despite what the Church has consistently taught, many people refuse to believe that the problems of the world are aided and abetted by the forces of the enemy. But the ravages of the battle are clear. Suicide is up, especially among young people. The drug culture is still growing. The institution of marriage is falling apart and children are out of control. It used to be that a strong Catholic or Christian home would be a strong enough safeguard to protect children from falling victim to things of the world and getting involved in gross sin. It's not the same anymore. Even in the strongest of Christian and Catholic homes children are getting into some very bad stuff and most often leaving the Church. One of the most distressing situations I have encountered over the years is the incredible remorse and sadness so many parents experience because their children have left the Church. A great number of the parents blame themselves. "What did we do wrong?" they will ask.

They have to be assured it is not their fault. I tell them to surrender their children every day to the Lord and to quote a particular verse of Scripture to the Lord. *If you take* [*your*] *delight in the*

Lord, he will give you the desires of your heart (Ps 37:4 RSV). "Image each one," I tell them, "on their faces in submission to God and thank him now for what he is going to do. He will come through for you." Why are these things happening today? Why are good, strong Catholic and Christian families not enough to keep the children faithful to God? I think it has to do with the weight of sin upon the world. Human society is tougher now than it was 20 years ago. It's much more challenging now for children. The assault of the enemy is fiercer. The pressure on children from their own peers is too much for mere human resources to combat. If we are thinking to ourselves: "Mine have turned out quite well," we should get down on our knees and thank God, day after day, for our blessings.

Perhaps the leaving of the Lord was preceded by different types of destructive behaviour—drugs, alcohol, sexual activity. The pressure to get involved in such stuff has a degree of intensity unknown to the previous generation.

Then there is the rise of Satanism and witchcraft. A couple of years ago I talked with a young man who had got involved in occult activity at age 17 with some of his buddies. They had gone out into the bush and engaged in some kind of strange ritual. At one point, they sat cross-legged in a circle and passed a candle around from one to the other. As the candle was held in front of each person a dark shadow from it was cast upon the earth although it was already night-time. The shadow was unexpected and quite out of the ordinary. And as the candle was passed from one to the other, the shadow would move too. Eventually it was my young friend's turn for the candle and the shadow. But when he passed the candle on to the next person, the shadow stayed in front of him. He was scared out of his mind. They all took to their heels. He denounced the whole thing and made a few resolutions. I hope he's kept them.

When I was teaching in high school, someone pointed out to me that one of the grade twelve girls was wearing a satanic cross—the crucifix upside down. I mentioned it to several other teachers on the staff and the reaction was disappointing. "That's just a phase she's going through, a fad, some said." Others said nothing and betrayed no real concern. Too bad. The whole thing is very real and has great potential for destruction.

One of the boys in the same class was an out-and-out satanist. "I don't care who knows it," he said. I asked: "Why are you into it? What has attracted you?" He said, "Satan has power. I've seen it and I like it."

The occult is fashionable, tantalizing, even enjoyable, but the price to be exacted is enormous. It takes us out of the presence of God forever. Satan's aim is to destroy, and in order to make that possible, first he entices.

Our response needs to be one of balance. One extreme is to see evil spirits everywhere. Seeing evil spirits around every corner is not healthy, but the other extreme is much more common. Satan's greatest deception is that he doesn't exist.

University courses now feature the occult. In fact, a couple of years ago in order to major in Religious Studies at a local university, one of the compulsory courses was witchcraft. It was taught by a woman who was a witch. She didn't hide it. She practised witchcraft.

Much of the occult activity going on today is lumped under the title "New Age". This comprises a long list of things: astrology, horoscopes, tea leaves, fortune tellers, the ouija board, tarot cards, seances, mediums, crystals, pyramid power, ESP, mental telepathy, SILVA Mind Control, telekinesis, spoon-bending, psychic healing, out-of-body experiences, subliminal tapes, spirit guides, the ascended masters, channeling. Shirley MacLaine, the well-known actress, is a current practioner in, and promoter of much of this.

New Age is not really an organized movement so much as it is a gathering of like-minded people. It came out of the counter-culture of the 1960's, was aided and abetted by mind-altering drugs, talk of the Aquarian Age, and the new world order. There's the notion that all potential lies within us and that self-actualization will somehow bring the best out of us: "There's a divinity in each of us. We are gods. No saviour is needed. We can save ourselves. There is no real sin in the world." Experience is made to be the important thing: "If it feels good, do it!"

The whole phenomenon is an obvious reaction to the dry intellectualism that characterized the so-called Age of Enlightenment, now shown to be bankrupt. New Age plugs into a real power. The power is not imaginary; it is quite available. Where does it come from? The power comes from the spirits of evil which can mimic the works of God: prophetic utterances, tongues, apparent miracles, healings. Just because a spiritual phenomenon occurs doesn't mean it's from God. It has to be carefully examined.

There's a war going on. As one preacher put it: "If we don't know we're in a war, we're already losing." How does it work? Every sin allows the enemy further access into the space that you and I live in. Not too long ago, I got a telephone call from a young man just as I was going in to the church to say the Saturday morning Mass. He said: "I need a priest. I'm going to die within minutes if I don't get some help." I did my best to sort out what he was trying to say. I got the impression that he'd been tampered with in some way. I got a couple of young men to go downtown and pick him up. They found him backed up against a wall at the corner of some building, paralyzed with fear. They prayed. They cast out spirits. They really didn't know what they were doing, but they did the best they could. The Lord seemed to give him some peace, and he calmed down a bit. Eventually, they brought him home, got him some food and let him sleep. This was followed by more prayer and deliverance. When I quizzed him later, I came to the conclusion he was definitely a victim of spiritual interference.

We don't have to look for the battle; we are in it. There are satanic altar calls at rock concerts. It's an ugly reality. The Age of Enlightenment has ended and people are searching for certainty and assurance, evidence and power, something that works. If we could just proclaim the Gospel and have people surrender to the Lord, they would find that the Lord's presence is something that works and brings peace. But the fascination with the occult and related activities continues.

The Scriptures are very clear, as has been the position of the Church from the beginning. *Do not go to mediums or consult fortune-tellers, for you will be defiled by them* (Lev 19:31). *Do not let your people practise divination or look for omens or use spells or charms, and do not let them consult the spirits of the dead.* (Deut 18:10 GNB). *He who practises divination and magic and consults fortune-tellers and mediums sins greatly against the Lord and stirs up his anger* (2 Chr 33:6 GNB). Satan is the Accuser (*cf.* Rev 12:10). Of Satan, Jesus says: He was a liar from the start; in fact, *he is the father of all lies* (John 8:44).

We are in a world that's messed up and might very well be getting messier. Human sin has allowed the spirits of evil entry to our lives. What are we supposed to do? Are we helpless in the face of it? The answer is 'No.' *I have given you power to tread upon snakes and scorpions and all the forces of the enemy,* says Jesus (Luke 10:19). Each individual believer has the power to overcome it. St. Paul writes: *The weapons of our warfare are mighty. With them we can pull down strongholds* (2 Cor 10:4 KJV). The weapons are the Word of God, the name of Jesus, Jesus' precious blood shed for the salvation of the world, the power of the Holy Spirit, the Rosary, blessed objects. St. Paul talks about the armour of God: *the belt of truth, the breastplate of justice, the shield of faith, the helmet of salvation, the footgear of zeal, and the sword of the Spirit, which is the Word of God* (*cf.* Eph 6:14-17).

These are the weapons. This is the armour. Ours is the victory. We don't have to be defeated.

Parents would be well advised to search out the Lord's protection on a regular basis for themselves and their children. They can pray for their children as they head off to school every day. They can anoint them with blessed oil or shake holy water over them. The battle is real and we need all the defenses the Lord makes available.

Jesus expelled evil spirits by a simple command. We are supposed to do the same in his name. If I get a sense that there's something suspicious happening in my life or around me that I can't explain, I command the spirits to be gone: "Spirit of rebellion [a common one today], be gone from here in Jesus' name." Some spirits have a deeper hold and are harder to expel. The Apostles once asked Jesus: Why could we not expel this one? His response was: *This kind does not leave* [*except*] *by prayer and fasting* (Matt 17:21).

During a retreat for priests in Steubenville in 1975 one of the speakers said that there are four ways that the spirits of evil can affect us.

1. Temptation. Temptations can come from the world or the flesh, of course, but they can also come from the spirits of evil as well. What are we supposed to do about them? We can take authority, command them to go. When faced with a temptation—to be greedy, for example—we can say: "Spirit of greed, be gone from me in Jesus' name." It can be done very quietly. Nobody even has to know we are doing it.

2. Oppression. This is external hassling, like ghosts or haunted houses or strange forces. The lives of the saints, particularly St. John Vianney, are instructive here. The saintly curé would be boiling a pot of potatoes on the stove and the water would jump out at him. The lamp would fall over onto his bed and set it on fire. This kind of thing doesn't happen too often, but it does happen. What are we supposed to do? Sometimes having Mass said in the place solves the problem. The prayers of the official ritual of the Church are likewise powerful. Blessed water, salt, and oil are additional ammunition.

3. Obsession. This is the situation where somehow a spirit of evil gets a foothold in an area of a person's personality—a dreadful temper that gets out of control, for example. Everything seems to be in rather good shape most of the time—a good and affable person—until something happens that causes the person to go wild, pounding the wall, and throwing objects. Does that mean it's an evil spirit of rage or anger? Not necessarily, but it could be. When a person's personality is involved, a ministry known as deliverance is called for. Oppression is external harassment. Obsession is internal.

4. Possession. Possession exists when an evil spirit resides in the body and exercises dominion over the body, and through it over the soul. It is very rare. In a Catholic setting, treatment of satanic possession requires the permission of the Bishop and the use of the official prayers of exorcism—a Catholic ritual that has been preserved down through the centuries. Every diocese is supposed to have an exorcist—one of the priests of the diocese who is called into situations where the ministry is required.

I'm convinced the enemy's main targets today are life, family and children, and the clergy. Look at the incidence of abortion, suicide, and violence. Marriage is on the rocks all over the place. Eleven- and twelve-year-olds are faced now with the same kind of things that fifteen- and sixteen-year-olds were faced with a generation ago. That's where the big battle is now—just as the youngsters are moving into junior high school. It's important for us to realize what the principal theatres of war are, so that the battle can be joined.

In the midst of all this stands the Church. In one place in the

Scriptures Jesus says: *I am the light of the world* (John 8:12). In another: *You are the salt of the earth and the light of the world* (*cf.* Matt 5:13-14). Yet, these days, we in the Church find ourselves in a weakened position, in a lot of ways not well equipped to deal with the war that's going on. We find ourselves badly divided, our energies largely diffused and misdirected. Have you noticed how often it is that people disagree with one another, and how much of our energies are directed to straightening things out? So often I find myself trying to harmonize people within the Church itself. Instead of being able to direct our energies outward into the fray bringing the Word of God to people who don't know it, serving the needy, and engaging in the spiritual war, our energies are directed inwards trying to sort ourselves out. We are divided.

My comments about the Church are not meant to be disloyal. I'm a Church man and I'll be part of it until the day I die. That's where the Lord has placed me and that's where I'm delighted to be. I love the Church even though it's on the ropes these days, even though it's wounded and limping. I love it with all its wrinkles and spots.

We have a scarcity of vocations to the priesthood and religious life. We have experienced an incredible falling away from the practice of the faith. The Church is not dead, but in many places it is largely asleep. A lot of us are clinging to the vague hope that somehow things will turn around. We've been lulled into thinking we can't do anything to change it anyway. We talk of cycles, of how things will bounce back somehow. We are paralyzed too often by false optimism. At St. Mary's the crowds are bigger than they used to be. Things are picking up. More people are getting involved. The collections are increasing. Glory to God, we say. That's great! Everything is fine. Everything is not fine! Everything is anything but fine. We have problems. We are not nearly as effective as we need to be. We are not taking territory for the Lord the way we could. We have to be more united and empowered by the Holy Spirit.

Within the Catholic Church today, many of our academics are in active rebellion against the Magisterium, the teaching office of the Church. This confuses people to no end and causes further divisions. Many of the scholars are saying that they are the 'New Magisterium'. The Bishops, they say, are not qualified to teach. Many of them are not great intellectuals. Teaching, they tell us, should be placed in the hands of the theologians since they are more enlightened and plugged into the latest research. The Church would be more relevant to the world if the academics were allowed to take charge, and prepare the Church of the future. Unfortunately, the teaching Church doesn't seem to know how to deal effectively with them. This is why I say the Church is in a weakened condition. Every time an attempt is made to bring some dissident into line, it becomes a media event. And the media line up in virtual unanimous accord behind the erring theologian. The media love to grasp every opportunity to blast away at the Church. The bad guys are never hard to identify. They are inevitably the Pope, and the Vatican authorities and Bishops that are solidly lined up with him.

There are some marvellous academics among us, but there's a large segment in the academic sphere teaching things that are directly opposed to the Magisterium. Here are some of the doctrines being falsely taught in the name of the Church by a whole amalgam of theologians and Scripture scholars:

- Jesus has left us the Church to run. He's not here now and we've got to run it ourselves.

- God does not intervene. We're on our own; so let's be brave and face it.

- World movements, such as of militant feminism and the gay movement, are being guided by the Holy Spirit.

- Scripture needs to be demythologized and re-understood. There are no miracles. The healing stories were included in the Gospels to make Jesus look good. They're symbolic at best.

- Jesus didn't really rise from the dead.
- There is no angelic or demonic realm. There is no devil.
- We need to re-evaluate and change some of our moral principles, particularly in the area of sexuality.
- Our number one task as a Church is to change the structures under which people live. That's the real evangelization.
- The Eucharist should be centred on the assembly of the people gathered, not on the elements of bread and wine. Christ is present in the people.
- We need to resist unjust regimes in the world, even to the assisted overthrow of governments.
- The only real sin is social.

These are not ideas of mine. These are the teachings of some theologians and other academics. They simply divide and weaken the Church.

It's interesting to note that, in this whole area, the Pope is regarded as 'out of touch'. Do we get the impression the Pope needs a new publicity director? He's lampooned again and again. He's said to be a victim of his Polish background, whatever that means. The dissenters have instant access to the media. All we have to do is try to censure one of them, and we've got a raging controversy on our hands.

It is also interesting to note that the congregations and religious orders involved in dissent are dying. They are not getting new members. I read a very strange statement incredible from a sister of one such congregation who said: "It's a good thing that no young girls are joining up with us, because the Church needs to learn the lesson that it can't count on slave labour anymore." Talk about head in sand!

Were the inspired writers of the New Testament addressing the academic community when they wrote what they did. *They [have] stultified themselves, speculating to no purpose. Their hearts have become darkened. They claim to be wise, but have turned into fools instead* (Rom 1:21-22). *Anyone who is so progressive that he does not remain rooted in the teaching of Christ, does not possess God* (2 John 1:9); *There is no other [gospel]... For even if we, or an angel from heaven, should preach to you a gospel not in accord with the one we delivered to you, let a curse be upon him* (Gal 1:7-8). The new agenda is hurting and will die. If we will stand by the true, authentic Magisterium, the Lord will stand by us.

So... we've come to the conclusion that the world is in bad shape. The Church is supposed to be able to turn that around and be the light of the world, but it is generally not in good shape either. Nonetheless, the Lord himself will not be defeated. I believe that renewal and revival are on their way. *The eyes of God range across the whole of the earth searching out those who are wholehearted for him, so that he might encourage them* (2 Chr 16:9 paraphrase). The Lord is looking for people today who will be faithful to him, who will line up with him, who won't compromise his Gospel.

I say again and again to the Lord: "I will do whatever you want. Although not really ready for much, I'm available. Use me any way you wish. I claim the protection of the blood of Jesus Christ, crucified on the Cross. I want to be empowered by the Holy Spirit. I want to be loyal to the Magisterium of the Church which I believe was founded by Jesus and has been faithful to his teachings right down through the centuries." That's where I want to be, and if I stand with other people who are there, too, then the Lord will be able to use us to help turn things around. I can see it happening. We need to be a people of hope who must not become discouraged by what we're up against.

This is not the Catholic Historical Society. This is the Church of the Living God. The Church may be limping at the moment, struggling here and there, but it is the Church that Jesus founded. The Church is not dead. And will not die. I sense the Lord is nudging us awake. Once the fire catches hold of enough of us then it will be: "Look out world! Here we come!"

Study Questions:

1 Why is it so important to honestly evaluate the present condition of the Church and the world?

2 Fr. Bob explains that the spiritual battle is very real. How can you protect yourself and those you love in the spiritual warfare that he describes?

3 Fr. Bob says, "I sense the Lord is nudging us awake. Once the fire catches hold of enough of us then it will be: 'Look out world! Here we come!'"

What has the Lord awakened in you? How has the fire caught hold of you?

CHAPTER ELEVEN

Ministry

Someone told me a few months ago that the ministries of the Church represent the 'third conversion'. The first is to the Lord Jesus himself and the second is to the Church that Jesus has founded. In other words, first we come to terms with Jesus. Then he leads us into the bosom of the Church. Once rooted in the body and taught and pastored a little bit, we hear the call to take on the burden of the Lord, and get involved in the ministries of the Church. It's the third conversion—past the "me and God" sort of comfortable phase of faith, past the sort of fascination with what God is doing, and into the harness in which the Lord can use us.

Not all people are capable of getting involved in the ministries of the Church, and that's fine. Some people need to spend more time working out the wounds in their own lives. For others, their young families are their principal ministry. For them to involve themselves extensively in the ministries of the Church would be out of order.

But the Lord can use us, even as we move within our limitations, no matter how weak we may seem to ourselves. If I consider myself weak, I am well qualified for God to work through me. *He has chosen the weak things of the world, so that he might confound the strong* (1 Cor 1:27 Douay). I consider myself weak, and I'm amazed that the Lord is able to work through me. I fought the notion for years that God could actually do something through me. I have had to come to terms with that, and acknowledge that the Lord has been able to use me. I continue to be amazed. The Lord can use any of us, even if we consider ourselves very weak.

Here is something written tongue-in-cheek by a fictitious body called The Galilee Psychological Testing Service, addressed to Rabbi Jesus Christ of Nazareth, Galilee:

> Several weeks ago, Sir, you requested that we give our series of psychological tests to the twelve men you were considering as possible associates in your work of ministry. Although we are still in the process of compiling the results of the tests, we thought you would be eager for a preliminary report.
>
> Hence, we are enclosing the test results for Mr. Simon bar Jonah [Peter, of course]. His profile sheet accompanies this letter. As you can tell, Mr. bar Jonah's personality is characterized by a dangerous rashness, overt pride, and a lack of emotional stability that would no doubt be detrimental to you and your work. We feel also that his general physical appearance would create a bad image for your proposed organization. Furthermore, during our research, we discovered that Mr. bar Jonah is, to put it bluntly, a bad fisherman. We suspect that his lack of success in his current employment is the cause of his willingness to leave all and follow you. Therefore, based on our testing, we highly recommend that you do not consider Mr. bar Jonah as a possible associate.

> We will make further recommendations regarding the fitness of the other eleven men as soon as possible, but in the meantime we can offer a few general observations. Mr. Philip wanted to know why the questionnaire was only in Greek and not also in Aramaic. "Wasn't Palestine a bilingual country?" he asked. Messrs. James and John Zebedee showed up for their appointment accompanied by their mother, a rather pushy person. To date, we have tested all except Mr. Thomas Twin. He, we believe, seriously doubts the validity of the process itself, and anyway he failed to show up for his appointment.
>
> Based on the evidence we have so far, we would recommend only Mr. Judas Iscariot, who has a fine head for financial matters, and would, no doubt, be a real asset to you and your organization.
>
> Sincerely,
>
> The Galilee Psychological Testing Service.

The point here is, of course, that the Lord does things his way and not ours. I was very shy in elementary and high school. For example, I seldom opened my mouth, never spoke in class, never put my hand up to answer a question even when I was quite sure I had the right answer. I didn't even know what my voice sounded like. In latter years I've done a lot of talking. After I spoke to a group of teachers a few years ago, a woman my age approached me with a question: "Aren't you the Bobby Bedard that lived on Third Avenue in Ottawa?" "Yes," I replied. "Well, I went to school with you," she said. She gave me her name. Sure enough, I remembered her. "Whatever happened to you?" she went on. "You were very quiet. You never spoke in class." "I know," said I, "But God got hold of me and went to work."

In my early days it is true: I never opened my mouth. Now it's never closed. The Lord can do what he wants with whoever is available to him.

Moses once asked God: *Who am I to go to the Pharaoh and bring the Sons of Israel out of Egypt* (Exod 3:11 RSV)? The Lord answered: *I will be with you* (Exod 3:12 RSV). In other words: What else do you need? Moses said: Why would you pick me? I'm old. [He was 80] I am slow of speech and tongue. I lack eloquence. The Lord told him it didn't matter. God didn't care, and told Moses to go ahead anyway.

Jeremiah said: *I am too young,* and the Lord responded: *Say not 'I am too young.' To whom I send you, you will go... Have no fear before them, because I [will be] with you to deliver you.* (Jer 1:6-8) Provided we say yes, God is committed to supplying whatever we don't have to allow us to do the things he wants us to do.

The general call to ministry goes with our commitment to the Lord, and comes from God. The very fact that we are baptized means that we are called to ministry within the Church. Pope John Paul II wrote an apostolic exhortation on the role of the lay person in the Church. He went on, page after page, telling the members of the Church that they are called to minister within the Church as a result of their Baptism. We are all called by the Lord to involve ourselves in his work on earth. The basic ministry of the Church falls upon all disciples.

Evangelization is the proclamation of the Good News, and the invitation to embrace it and to live it. It is the Church's number one mandate. This is the call from Jesus himself to the Church that he has founded. In each of our own lives—at work, home, or school—we are to bring the Good News. We are to bring the Gospel to the ends of the earth.

In 1975 Pope Paul VI wrote an encyclical on the evangelization of the nations titled *Evangelii Nuntiandi (On Evangelization in the Modern World)*. He considered it the best thing he ever wrote. "The Church exists," he says, "to evangelize." He said we had to recover within the Church the charism of evangelization. The present Holy Father has said that our principal task today as a

Church is to evangelize the baptized.

Sometimes I find that Catholics are uncomfortable with the very word 'evangelization'. It conjures up for them the image of impassioned oratory on television. I remember being on a diocesan commission on evangelization, a group of about eight. Right at the start, one of the religious sisters present said: "I'll be up front with you. I don't like the term 'evangelization'. It sounds too Protestant. I have lots of respect for Protestants, but we're Catholics." In *Evangelii Nuntiandi*, Pope Paul wrote that evangelization is our ministry, our work. Evangelization is a Catholic word and should be the number one Catholic work. We have to bring it back to the heart of the Church now and give it its proper place of prominence. As it is, we are a Church that tries hard to carry out the rest of the Lord's mandate as well as we can. But we don't evangelize very much. The falling away from the Church of so many baptized Catholics is the result of our not evangelizing our own people. We have not called them to come to terms fully with Jesus. We have not challenged our people to make themselves completely available to the Lord.

Besides evangelization, we are called to teach, to disciple people, to console, to counsel, to listen, to pray, to worship, to celebrate and to serve the disadvantaged. That's a long list of duties, and we've done them reasonably well. We've built institutions for the hungry and the homeless. We've ministered all over the place. But we have not called people to surrender their lives to the Lord. We are paying the price for not doing that.

Evangelization is not the Church's only ministry or work, but it is number one. The Church is in decline. Numbers are way down.

Is there any practical way of telling whether or not specific people are evangelized? I believe so. My firm conclusion is that there will be some clear characteristics in their lives:

They will be enthused about God and his Word and his work.
They will have a hunger to understand the Word of God.
They will want to be involved with the life of the Church.
They will have a desire to share and to witness to what God has done in their own lives.
Their conversation will be sprinkled with references to God.
They will not be uncomfortable talking about something they think the Lord may have done in their lives, or may be saying to them.
They will be enthusiastic worshippers.

Those are people who are well evangelized. They're not perfect by any means. They may, be lacking in wisdom and sensitivity. As one young priest, whom I know quite well, puts it: "When people are first evangelized, they should be locked up for six months." He's got a point. Very often these people tend to guilt trip others, as though they have something the rest of us don't have. Pestering others is bad news. It turns people off—the very opposite effect to the one intended.

Becoming super-spiritual is a very poor witness, too. Sometimes evangelized people begin to take themselves too seriously. God is speaking to them. They are getting 'words' from him, quite often for others. They get hung up on 'prophetic' messages from all over, usually of a gloom and doom nature. Visions and apparitions can begin to outrank Mass and the Sacraments in importance. Not good. The Church wants us to move very slowly in these areas.

In fact, we are really not meant to be spiritual at all. If God had wanted us to be spiritual, he'd have made us angels. As St. Irenaeus, one of the early fathers of the Church, said: "The glory of God is man [woman] fully alive." We're created human, intended to be filled with joy, fervour, enthusiasm for God's work, a zest for living, and an optimistic viewpoint.

How does one evangelize? The process is almost too simple:

1. The Good News (God's love and plans for us) is proclaimed or shared.

2. The Good News is accepted, said "Yes" to.

3. The Holy Spirit goes to work and begins to change the person who has made a positive response, who has invited God to take over his/her life.

There are three people involved in the evangelization:

1. The disciple who evangelizes.

2. The person who hears and responds.

3. The Holy Spirit.

Evangelization is, therefore, something that we start and that God finishes. When the person hears the Word and responds positively, God begins the transformation. The churches that understand and are faithful to this whole dynamic, who make it their number one ministry, are the ones that are flourishing and growing.

But it's not a one-shot deal. Instant conversions can be real, but often they don't last. Conversions have to be followed up, a process that requires the support of a believing community. There has to be a continual discipling process. There's a great deal to be learned. People who have been evangelized or 'converted' need now to be taught, pastored, and discipled and later integrated into some ministry within the Church.

How effective is our Catholic educational system? At the end of high school are our sons and daughters evangelized? Do they know the Lord? Probably not. What we do in our schools, and very often within the Church at large, is put the cart before the horse. We teach all kinds of things, but we don't evangelize.

One of the priests at Madonna House in Combermere, Ontario,

Fr. Bob Wild, puts it this way: We have to question our capacity to teach anybody anything until that person is to some degree evangelized. His book, *The Post-Charismatic Experience*, makes for very interesting reading. In other words, we have to start calling people to the Lord. Once that happens effectively and people open their lives to God, then they are ready to be taught. I found that in my own twenty years of teaching high school, I didn't begin to evangelize my students until about my fifteenth year. The difference was like night and day. Those who responded couldn't learn enough. They had a hunger to know about God. They began going to Mass and the Sacraments and reading the Bible. I had to move fast to keep up with them.

The purpose of evangelization is conversion. Evangelization is a ministry. Conversion is a grace. We don't convert people. God does. He calls us to be faithful, to do what he wants us to do—to evangelize—and then he gives the grace.

A priest who works for the American Bishops puts it this way: "Catechesis, or teaching, presumes that the evangelization, the conversion process, has already taken place. It presupposes the person has accepted Jesus Christ as Lord in accord with age, or state in life." This is an official document coming out of Washington from the U.S. Catholic Conference.

In addition to evangelizing, we have to care for people as well. We have to be aware of God's little ones, the 'anawim': the sick, the lonely, the neglected, abused children and women, the elderly, the abandoned, the addicted, those in bondage. We have to be mindful of those who are in need, and try to relate their neediness to our own situation today. At St. Mary's Church in Ottawa we try to respond to these needs. We visit the sick. We visit those who need food. We try to serve immigrants. We support the local food bank and a soup kitchen and shelter downtown. We have a social action ministry, we support a drop-in centre.

Ten years ago, I was present at a meeting of the priests of the diocese where the Bishop was introducing a new program. It sounded good, but he sensed their spirits sagging as they listened to him outlining his idea. This was confirmed by their questions: "Bishop, we are already overworked. How can we possibly put another program into operation?" The Bishop's response was: "Father, you must not assume that all the gifts for ministry within the Church belong to you, the priest. Many of the gifts are in the pews."

Another one of the brethren said: "But, Bishop, people won't volunteer. Every January I put out a sheet of things to be done, ministries for people to sign up for, and the response is very poor."

Of course, yours truly had to put in a word: "Your Grace, I think that asking for volunteers is not the way to get people into ministry. We have to identify the people with the gifts and call them forth." He pointed at me and said: "That's absolutely right." Yet another of the clergy said: But people don't know how to do anything. They need training. And to be very honest, it would take longer for me to train them than it would to do the things myself." Yours truly again: "Maybe we need some kind of facility, Bishop, whereby people can get training for lay ministry within the Church." "Wonderful idea," he said. A school of lay ministry was to be established. Three guesses who got the job!

Ministry to youth is a very difficult one. When I was first setting up the lay school, I circulated a questionnaire that listed a series of ministries including ministry to youth. The first question was: "Rate the following ministries in order of importance in your opinion." The second question was: "Rate the same ministries in the order of how you would feel your gifts would fit in, or where you would see yourself involved." Youth ministry registered number one on the list of importance, and last on the list of where people saw their own gifts being effective. What were they saying? They were clearly saying that people are desperate to find something that can work for their children, but they haven't got the slightest idea of what to do.

Youth are tough to reach in our day. They belong to a distinct sub-culture, one very difficult to understand. The 'problem' in reaching young people is seen by many as a high priority.

I'm no expert, but I have taught high school, and have had a lot of experience with the young. The subculture today has an incredible power to bend youngsters to its own purposes. It can almost force them into conformity: experimentation with drugs, drinking, sex, the occult. These are not God's ways. They will not really satisfy people or fulfill their longings.

We are in a war, a spiritual battle. One of Satan's prime targets is young people, even children. We don't understand the intensity of the combat. Formerly, the believing family was strong enough to resist the world. Not so today. Many families are in agony because some or all of their children are victims of the war.

We have to understand that it's not our fault. We do the best we can. The intensity of the battle has been turned up several notches. The enemy's hand and strategy are very clear: knock down the family, get after the kids, and destroy as much life as possible. That is where the whole abortion holocaust comes in. Abortion is an attack on the most defenceless of human beings—the unborn. What are we supposed to do about all this? Human strategies won't work. We have to get involved with the power of God. We need to draw commitment from people, including the very young. Concerted prayer and corporate fasting are things most people can get involved in. And we have to step up our support for people who work long hours every week for the cause of life.

There is a difference between the ministry that I do as an ordained priest and the ministry that everybody else is called to be involved in as members of the Church. In one way, clerics and laity have similar responsibilities: to evangelize and to promote the Kingdom of God. But, in a lot of other ways, our ministries are different.

The Companions of the Cross, of which I am a part, have a body of teachings that we consider very basic. A few years ago, the coordinators of the community felt that I should spend as much of the summer as possible writing these out. So I got myself a little word processor, and for six or seven weeks, every Monday after Mass I went away, returning every Friday afternoon. I spent the entire week writing. According to the computer, I wrote 70,000 words. These things have all been put together in a little volume that bears the title, *We are Called to be Companions of the Cross*. God's written Word—the Bible—is properly called 'the sacred writings'. We refer to our modest effort as the not so sacred writings—the NSSW.

Here is the section that I wrote on the priesthood:

> If there is concern about defining the role of the priest within the Church today, we have simply to look to Jesus himself—*The Eternal High Priest* (Heb 6:20 NLT). A priest will do whatever Jesus did. Jesus was a father to his flock. He made visible the Fatherhood of God to his people. He shepherded them. A priest must do the same. We need to see the priest as the father-substitute that God appoints for his family on earth.
>
> It's not easy to be a father today. The great masses of physically and emotionally absent fathers have served to produce a largely unfathered people. Men, in general, are not in good shape. Saving the many delightful exceptions, we could probably make a rather good case for a crisis of masculinity in our time. Males, the statistics tell us, account for 75% of all suicides, 88% of all arrests for drunk driving, and are the subjects of six of seven drug-

related charges. We don't have accurate numbers, but the percentage of men who are in regular attendance at church is much lower than the record of women. Into this constituency of God's people, who are to a great extent either inadequately fathered or not fathered at all, steps the priest. It will not be easy for him to father these people, and yet that is what he must do. He must do what Jesus did.

Everything else that the priest is to do must flow from his role as father to God's flock. He will preside over family occasions, liturgical or otherwise. He will affirm his people, calling them as any good father must do, into their true identity as sons and daughters of God. He will bless and anoint them. He will represent them before the throne of God, standing as a mediator and pleading their cause. He will seek the direction of God himself. He will then proclaim the word of the Lord and call others to embrace it, and live it out. He will call people to specific ministries within the Body of Christ, prepare them to fulfill the tasks, mandate them in the name of the Lord, and send them out to serve God's purposes. He will encourage them, support them, be a steadying influence for them, be their rallying point. He will call them forth when they step out of line, correct them, absolve them, and heal their wounds. He will rejoice with them in their good times, and grieve with them in their sorrows. All these things Jesus did. All these things a father must do. This is the priest's mandate.

A priest's job will also include catching the Lord's vision for his people. He will need all the input they can give him, and he will have to spend lots of time trying to hear the Lord's word in prayer. He will involve himself in the Church's principal mission—the proclamation of God's Good News of life in Christ—and take the lead preaching in season and out, calling all who will listen to turn their lives over to the Lord. In his own person, he will represent God's people everywhere he goes.

It is very easy for a priest to get caught up with other things. He must resist the temptation. When the Apostles found that their attention was being more and more taken up with worldly things, they moved quickly to a solution. They delegated others to do a lot of the daily tasks so that they themselves could concentrate upon *prayer and the service of the Word* (Acts 6:4 JB), leaving them freer to shepherd the Lord's flock. They were not to be tyrannized by the urgent as so many of us priests tend to be today.

In order for the Lord's family—the Church—to function according to his plan, the priest must first fulfill the role designated for him. He must have a clear notion of who and what he is to be, but he must not take over the tasks that the Lord has in mind for others. Just as a father is not meant to co-opt all family functions, neither must the priest. In fact, the Church at any level does not accomplish what it is supposed to, according to the plan of God, when the priest over-functions and usurps the roles of others.

Just as it is clear what the priest is to be and do, so it is likewise clear what he is to entrust to others. He is not to be an administrator. It is probably best if somebody else knows, where the keys are, adds up the columns of figures, deals with the bank, calls the plumber, buys the food, writes the cheques, locks and unlocks the church, and turns off the lights. The priest is not a details man. Let him immerse himself in prayer and God's Word, and beg the Lord for his vision and direction.

The priest is not a counsellor. He is not the answer to everybody's problem. In my experience, a great majority of people who are convinced that they have to speak to a priest don't really have to at all. They may certainly need to talk, but my conviction is that other people will have more gifts from God in the area of counselling than will priests. Part of the priest's own charism will be to identify the gifts in others—to call them forth, to prepare them for ministry, to send them out, and to support them.

He is not an organizer. It is better if he does not put the parish picnic and potluck suppers together. And hopefully he will find that other people are much better at conducting meetings and more efficient at setting up parish council elections. The priest is not a sacristan, a porter, an office manager or decorator. It is not that these tasks are below him; it is just that they are not his tasks.

When we get right down to it, most of the Church's ministries are proper not to the priest at all, but to lay people. They can counsel, organize, administer, teach, prepare children for the Sacraments, instruct adults in the faith, conduct marriage preparation programs, run meetings, decorate the church, plan the liturgies, lead the music, conduct devotions and para-liturgical services, visit the sick, the lonely, the elderly and those in prison, feed the hungry, house the homeless, rescue the abandoned, take up the Church's great causes of life, justice and peace, minister to young people of all ages, minister to families in trouble, form prayer teams for intercession and inner healing. The list could go on and on.

The family of God is out of order and doesn't function to his plan when the priest tries to involve himself in doing things that other people are called to do. But let's not be too quick to fault him. After all, he is the man on the spot, the one with the highest profile among God's people, the one who most often finds himself in the eye of the storm. This is understandable, considering the tradition of people turning to him for everything, and expecting that he would have all the answers. It is so easy for him to be captured by the immediate need. However, if he allows himself to be drawn into things he should stay out of, he will either neglect the work that he is supposed to do (prayer and service of the Word), or he will burn out trying to do everything.

Speaking only for myself, I'd have to say that the training I received years ago for my role as a priest among God's people did not prepare me very well at all for what I now see I am supposed to do. I think most of my contemporaries would agree. We were not trained to work with teams of lay people, the people who would do the sensitive ministry with us. Rather, we understood that we were to do our best to meet whatever needs people might have. We were to involve ourselves in continual crisis response. Ours was to be a ministry of availability.

I believe we have to be faithful to Vatican II, to rethink all of that, and begin to see it very differently. I am convinced that our priority as priests must be to see what God is doing, and to minister to that.

This may very well be a time of God's special visitation. There are many indications that he is releasing the power of his Holy Spirit in greater and greater measure. God is on the move. He is doing the initiating. We have to recognize his initiatives, point them out to our people, and seek the Lord as to how best we are to react. If we let him, he will do the acting; it will be for us to do the reacting.

The priest is to be a blessing to his people. God can do wondrous things through those whom he appoints as heads over the many segments of his family. He has said so himself: *I will lavish choice portions on the priests, and my people shall be filled with my blessings* (Jer 31:14).

> The life of a priest is not always an easy one, but there is truly nothing quite like it. There is nothing like watching God go to work. As priests, we are privileged to be right in the front line, involved in the thick of the action. If I had to do it all over again, I'd do exactly the same thing—I'd become a priest.
>
> Are there any young, or not so young, men considering a call to the priesthood today? Let them consider it well; it's an exciting time to be a priest. The Lord is doing something very special in our day. He has initiated a thoroughgoing renewal of the whole Church, and he is calling men from the four corners of the Church into the priesthood, men whom he will train to lead the way. Anyone whom the Lord may be tapping on the shoulder would do well not to miss the call.
>
> Jesus related to his disciples as a father to his family. A priest must do the same. It is not so strange, then, that we all call him 'Father'.

Those are my reflections on the priesthood. Can we see the distinction? The priest is called out from among his people and ordained. Hands are laid upon him: *Stir into a flame the gift of God bestowed upon you when my hands were laid upon you* (2 Tim 1:6). Timothy was called forth to be a father to God's people. He was ordained.

There is a qualitative difference between the ordained ministry and the ministry of the whole Church. Nonetheless, we must not overemphasize the ordained ministry so that the ministry of the whole Church somehow falls into disrepair. Above all, the priest is the one who presides at the Eucharist. He is the one who confects the sacrament. He is the one who stands in the sandals of Jesus, and says Jesus' words: "This is my Body, and this is my Blood." He is the one who is set aside for that. He presides. He calls people into ministry. Everybody has a call into the ministry of the Church. We all have different gifts.

I didn't make myself a priest. My priesthood was authentic only when I was called. I thought I heard the Lord calling me to be a priest. I offered myself; I went through the seminary. They didn't throw me out. They put me forward for ordination. But only at the moment that the Bishop called me did I know that my vocation to the priesthood was authentic. Our call to ministry within the Church is authentic only when we are called. We can't just say: "The Lord is calling me to do this." We can't just go ahead and do it. It has to fall within the structure of the Church that the Lord himself has founded.

The Lord calls us all to be in submission. I'm in submission to the Bishop. The members of a parish are in submission to the pastor. There isn't any ministry that's carried out in the name of the Church in a parish setting that's authentic unless the pastor calls it into being.

Ministry is the exchange of burdens. Jesus says: *Come to me, all you who labour and are* [*heavily*] *burdened, and I will refresh you ... for my yoke is* [*easy*] *and my burden light* (Matt 11:28 Douay). In other words: "My burden is the conversion of the world. If you offer yourself to me, I will place you into my harness and give you the tools and the brothers and sisters to do my work." It's a call to all believers.

For more information on this series and other Lay Formation core formation programs, please visit: ***companionscross.org***

Corresponding DVD's featuring Fr. Bob Bedard, and Study guides are available. Please contact us at ***1.866.885.8824***

View The Catholic Disciple *videos and find group resources online at:* ***thenewevangelist.com***

COMPANIONS OF THE CROSS

We are a Roman Catholic community of priests, committed to living and ministering together as brothers in the Lord. God has called us to labour boldly for the renewal of the Church through a dynamic evangelization centered upon Christ crucified, who is God's power and wisdom. Spurred on by the love of God, we desire all people to come into the fullness of life through a personal and ongoing encounter with Jesus Christ.

Spirituality

LOVE FOR CHRIST CRUCIFIED, A SPIRITUALITY OF GOD'S POWER AND WISDOM | Jesus's death on the cross and resurrection saved the world. Therefore, we fully commit ourselves to him; seek his will in all we do; and trust in his power to do it.

"We proclaim Christ Crucified...the Power of God and the Wisdom of God"
(1 Cor. 1:23-34)

WE ARE:

- Men of the Eucharist
- Led and empowered by the Holy Spirit
- Truly devoted to Mary
- Loyal to the Magisterium

Brotherhood

LOVE FOR ONE ANOTHER, A LIFE OF TRUE BROTHERHOOD
We base ourselves on the model of Jesus and his disciples, who lived together, ministered together, and supported one another.

Mission

LOVE FOR THE CHURCH, A MISSION OF EVANGELIZATION AND RENEWAL | We invite all people into an initial and ongoing encounter with Jesus. As we are transformed by his love, we bring about authentic renewal in the Church and world.